INTENTION!

INTENTION!

USING THE NEW SCIENCE BEHIND THE LAW OF ATTRACTION TO CREATE YOUR BEST LIFE NOW

MATHIAS WADE

Giant Squid Publishing

Published by Giant Squid Publishing

ISBN: 978-1-9768-8083-4

Typesetting services by BOOKOW.COM

To my grandma Della who passed during the writing of this book. Thank you for sharing your beautiful life with us.

Acknowledgments

I couldn't have finished this book without the love and support of amazing family and friends.

Thank you to Christiane Knerr for reading and re-reading the initial drafts and providing valuable feedback.

Thank you to the following additional pre-readers who offered important feedback: Michael Platt, Zac Robinson, Jason Cheek, and to Reid Allen for valuable editing of the first drafts while on military deployment.

CONTENTS

Introduction

Recently I was returning from a weekend trip to Iceland where I ran a half marathon and went exploring with a group of friends. On the flight back home, I sat next to an older gentleman and experienced one of the most engaging and interesting conversations of my life. This man was a research professor at a university in Reykjavik and had been studying human social behavior for the majority of his life. What was so interesting was his approach to the study, which was purely grounded in strict mathematics. Magnusson (a very Icelandic name) was using mathematical formulas to understand how humans interacted. He had spent his entire life devoted to understanding the wide diversity of human behaviors such as courtship, group psychology, sports, and any and every aspect of human behavior. Behind every human action, he explained, was an algorithm which could accurately predict what a person or group would do. In other words, he felt that our lives were entirely deterministic. We held opposing views, which spurred a lengthy debate. In the end, he invited me to attend a conference with him at Wurzburg University in Germany at which he was the keynote speaker. For several days after our discussion my mind was busy with thoughts and I found myself waking up in the middle of the night with a strong need to write down my feelings. Many of the concepts we discussed during that three-hour flight from Reykjavik to Frankfurt have found their way into this book. This man confessed to me that after a lifetime of study that he found no ultimate purpose for human existence. He described how he had suffered a stroke three years prior and nearly passed away in the ambulance on the way to the hospital. He said that while he was laying there dying, he simply thought "This is the end and this isn't a bad way to go." He said that he had no regrets and that he did not have any miraculous epiphanies when he came to in the hospital the next day. He did say something that struck a chord with me however. He said the only fear that he had was that he would likely die an ignorant man, ignorant of mankind's true meaning and purpose. With his many years of study in the sciences and mathematics, he was unable to draw any concrete conclusions about our natural world that might help him decipher man's ultimate reason for being.

Science can tell us much more than just *how* to function in the natural world. Science also has the potential to tell us *why*. As we examine our reality and as we analyze every piece of information that science provides us, we can start to put the puzzle pieces together and form a narrative that describes our true purpose. I believe that nature and the universe have provided us plenty of gentle clues that point toward our divine purpose. Most often, these bits of data are blatantly ignored because they don't fit within the neat and tidy box that we know as the scientific method.

Let's step outside that box and allow ourselves to take the hints that the universe provides and put together a story of meaning and truth. This story explains more than just how, it explains why we exist. When you experience personal hardship, fall in love, experience joy, or feel a deep connection with nature you are experiencing non-tangible aspects of the human experience. Our science cannot explain these beyond describing them as a series of complex neuro chemical reactions which occur in the brain. Our science reduces them to a series of biological processes or more blatantly ignores these experiences all together.

The truth is all aspects of human experience are equally valid — both tangible and non-tangible. Emotions, feelings, and spiritual phenomenon are elements of our existence that add to the evidence supporting a story which depicts humans as spiritual creatures, on a grand journey of growth and discovery.

If you've never been exposed to the concepts of an egoic self and the true self then this book will be life changing for you. If you have some experience with meditation, prayer, or spiritual health then this book will help you to develop techniques to live a happier and more mindful life free from the burdens of negative energy. The concepts discussed in this book are purely non-denominational and do not adhere to any particular theology or dogma. All information has been built on a foundation of spiritual knowledge spanning thousands of years from varied and disparate sources such as Buddhism, Christianity, Eastern and Western philosophy and modern science. My personal experiences have shaped much of the material and I include many stories from my life to illustrate certain points. I sincerely hope that as you read through each chapter you will connect with your own experiences. Completing the exercises throughout the book will help with this immensely. You will learn life is an amazing adventure of your own making. This book will give you the knowledge and understanding to achieve real and lasting peace and happiness starting right now in this present moment.

Do you constantly obsess over your problems? Do you worry to the point of exasperation? Are you mired in pain, self-doubt, fear of the future, or an overwhelming desire to have something more? Feelings of lack, wanting and discontent are products of a mind controlled by ego. We have the capacity to overcome these obstacles to happiness through mindfulness. Understanding why we obsess over the future or the past helps us to triumph over our pain. Embracing emotions rather than suppressing them allows us to process and appreciate them simply as byproducts of a thinking mind. Mindfulness turns the volume down on our emotions. It is the ultimate form of self-regulation. Through mindfulness we become free to act boldly and with purpose because we are no longer hindered by obsessive and negative thoughts.

Let's work together on this journey of self-discovery to change our thinking and our lives. Once we've achieved a certain level of mindfulness we are then fit enough to start creating our reality as we choose. You alone are the creator and this book will give you the tools to achieve whatever it is you desire. Your mind is the ultimate machine of creation!

CHAPTER 1: THE POTENTIAL

"Impossible is just a big word thrown around by small men who find it easier to live in the world they've been given than to explore the power they have to change it. Impossible is not a fact. It's an opinion. Impossible is not a declaration. It's a dare. Impossible is potential. Impossible is temporary. Impossible is nothing." – Muhammad Ali

On a sweltering hot day in Southern Mississippi in the year 1818, a little girl was born on a cotton plantation to slave parents. Biddy, as she came to be known, grew up under the love and direction of her parents until one day, being old enough to work, she was removed without warning from her home and sent off to auction to be sold. The little girl grew to be a lovely young woman; strong, smart, and curious about the world. In 1836, at the age of eighteen, Biddy was given away as a birthday present to a new owner. Having recently converted to Mormonism, her new owner decided to immigrate to the Utah territory in order to settle in with a newly established Mormon community. Biddy was forced to walk over 2,000 miles behind her owner's wagon with their cattle during the trek, all the while working for free to care for the master's young children.

Shortly after reaching the Utah territory, Biddy's master decided again to relocate his family and slaves to the San Bernardino, California area in order to start up a new Mormon community. Again Biddy was forced to walk behind the family wagon with the animals, over grueling mountain passes and searing endless deserts.

In California, the anti-slavery movement was in full swing, and thanks to a kind hearted local sheriff who persuaded a local judge to free her, she was granted full emancipation on January 21, 1856. Biddy had never had a last name, and now as a free woman she took the last name of Mason, because this was the middle name of the mayor of San Bernardino at the time.

Biddy Mason worked for ten years and saved everything she earned until in 1866 she had accumulated a total $250 in savings. Although this doesn't sound like much by today's standards, it was enough to enable her to purchase two small pieces of land in downtown Los Angeles. On one lot she built a small house that she lived in until the day she died. The other lot she rented out as a source of income. At this point in her life Biddy Mason had secured her freedom, owned her home debt free, and had become financially independent.

For a formerly illiterate slave to have achieved this level of success was unheard of in 1860s America. However, Biddy Mason wasn't content to stop there. Her dreams outweighed her obstacles, and she continued to manifest success in her life. Through swift and intelligent real estate decisions, Biddy went on to become one of the wealthiest women in Los Angeles. At the time of her death, she was worth over $7.5 million dollars in today's money. Additionally, she became known as an active philanthropist and a highly respected member of the Los Angeles community.

Despite what the world told Biddy Mason she should believe about herself and society, she chose to believe only what empowered her to reach her goals. She knew that the beliefs the world held at the time about blacks and women weren't in line with the grand vision she had for herself. Her courageous and beautiful story is a shining example of the potential we have to overcome

the limiting beliefs the world feeds us, as well as the limiting beliefs we choose to accept about ourselves. Biddy Mason led a
deliberate life — full of abundance, hope, and unwavering faith.

I tell you this story because it brings to light two natural tendencies of humans; one bad and one good. Institutions such as
slavery arose from the minds of men whose egos were buried deep
in their sense of superiority. This superiority was supported by
the science, religion, and nationalism of the day. People naturally
tend to think they are in a superior group and will use all means
of power available to support this falsehood. The good part of
the story is the human mind, when used to harness the power of
the Law of Attraction, can overcome even the strongest of evil
forces arising from the egos of men.

Oftentimes books about the Law of Attraction will give advice
such as *"generate the feelings of having it now"* and *"cultivate a spirit
of gratitude"*. You'll also find such advice in this book but you'll
find much, much, more than just pragmatic words — I will tell
you exactly *why* such advice works. We can both hack the system
and use pragmatic Band-Aids to achieve results or we can take
the time to understand deeply the theory and reasoning behind
such advice. Knowing the *"how and whys"* enables us to achieve a
state of constant and continual manifestation and joy in our lives.

The Law of Attraction works best when we are completely and
totally aligned with the spiritual energy of the universe. Sounds
deep right? It's actually pretty simple. Take a moment and think
about the last time you were alone in nature - perhaps you were on
a camping trip or a run in the woods. Did you experience a peaceful feeling watching the tress rock back and forth in the wind?
Did you feel an underlying connection to something greater than
yourself as you listened to the waves crash along the shoreline of
a lake? These types of experiences in nature are an easy way for
us to experience the energy and flow of a universal force. Peace,
love, perfection, acceptance, and solitude are some of the words

we might use to describe the feelings that arise when we connect with nature. We can also experience universal energy when meditating—even more intensely and deeply than we can in the natural world.

In order to receive what you want in life, be it a new car, a loyal and supportive group of friends, a restored marriage, lasting love, health, or limitless wealth, you and the universe have to be on the same page. If you are using the Law of Attraction from the position of the false self or ego, you will find that it will only work infrequently or not at all. You may even find that the opposite of what you want manifests in your life. If you are using the Law of Attraction with purely ego-based intent, you may actually bring hardship or suffering into your life. Why is this? Quite simply, the universe knows what's best for you. If you are experiencing suffering or hardship, it's because that's exactly what you need right now in your life in order to grow and learn as a spiritual being.

As you read, your mind will be primed to move toward a way of thinking that is in line with the universal energy and power flow of infinite intelligence. First, you need to understand the concept of ego and the false self and why our motivations oftentimes arise from it. Secondly, you will learn to understand how our emotions play into the need for ego validation with the false self. Third, you learn techniques to reduce your connection to your false self.

Once you have this foundation, we are going to jump quickly into the modified Law of Attraction manifestation techniques I have developed. While operating from the true self and getting fired up through directed and inspired action, you will manifest continually and predictably. Additionally, your manifestation goals will never harm others but to the contrary will result in a state of charitable abundance for all those whom you come into contact. Your life will blossom, as will the lives of all those who choose to be receptive to the unlimited source of power and universal love that will radiate from within your being once you and the universe are in pure and complete alignment. Don't worry, the process is simple.

Defining the Problem: Life as a Modern Human

In modern society, we are born into a world which teaches us from an early age to construct an identity based on assigned labels and various external factors. We are told as children that we are white, black, Christian, Muslim, Jewish, etc. We are taught that along with these labels, we hold a set of values and beliefs which serve to identify us to others in this world. Above all, we are taught to distinguish and differentiate ourselves from others. More often than not, we are told that our identify is *better* than others.

As we grow older, the idea of identity and distinction from others is constantly reinforced. We are fed a cornucopia of false information about ourselves. We are told that we are better if we wear a certain brand of clothes, that we are more valuable if we have lots of beautiful friends, that we are more worthwhile if we drive a shiny new car or live in a nice neighborhood.

When you were born into this world, naked and crying, your identity was already fully formed and present. The addition of external objects, people, and labels did not change your identity but rather worked to construct and define a false self. This false identity is the sanctuary of the ego and ultimately is a source of complete heartache and hopelessness. You will never find solace, peace, and happiness in the false self. The identity you were born with is free from labels and external things. You have the ability to return to your true self and cut ties with the bonds of enslavement which the ego uses to trick you into believing that your identity merely consists of a conglomeration of possessions and things.

The New Dark Age

Imagine sitting around a campfire with your family: your grand-parents, cousins, nephews and nieces, and many of your closest friends. There's no television around to occupy your time. There's no internet or smartphones available to check your social media status. In order to pass the time and to provide some entertain-ment your grandpa stands up and tells a story of times past. Ev-eryone is intrigued to hear his account of what it was like to live through the war years and everyone tries their best not to cry when he talks about how he met your grandma. Perhaps you and your family group are out in a wilderness area, without access to the food and shelter that modern society normally provides rather easily. Your days together might involve foraging for food, hunting wild game, or building shelters for the older folks. The children spend their days playing outside in nature. After a long hard day, the group comes together again to share a meal in front of the fire, talk for hours, and share stories about their day.

This scenario pretty much describes human existence for the ma-jority of world history. Do you think that anyone in this scenario would ever say they were lonely? Would anyone in this scenario slip into chronic depression or anxiety? Would anyone in this sce-nario foster ill-will and jealousy for other members of the group? Almost undoubtedly, not.

Living in a close community feels incredibly comforting and safe. We evolved as humans to be deeply interconnected. Throughout most of human history, you would have lived in close proximity to others and have been able to talk to someone close to you about any fears, anxieties, or problems that you might experience. As technology has advanced over the centuries, it has enabled us to move further and further away from the interconnected life that we once experienced in the past.

As humans, we have evolved to survive and flourish within a tight-knit community. Throughout most of human history, we've had to rely on one another just for simple survival. Belonging to a group is hard-wired into our DNA. We are not just social creatures, we are hyper-social creatures, highly dependent on belonging to a community in order to thrive and reach our full potential. As technology has been introduced throughout mankind's history, it has had the effect of making our lives easier, more comfortable, and longer. The biggest drawback to this is that it also allows us to become more and more autonomous and seemingly less dependent upon one another.

It's easy to disconnect from our communities in this modern age. Our diversions serve to give us a temporary illusion of connectedness and community. Social media gives us the appearance of connectedness, but it will never be able to replicate the feeling of total inclusion and acceptance that we once felt; sitting around a fire sharing a meal with your tribe. Later in this book we will discuss how connecting to social groups will magnify your ability to manifest abundance and joy in your life. Having a supportive group of friends is essential to total actualisation as a human being.

Everywhere we can see the signs of a world living within their egos. Dogma, political beliefs, discrimination, and hate are used to justify the oppression of others. In extreme cases people are killed as a result of ideological divisions.

The twentieth century saw a level of death and destruction beyond anything imaginable in human history. The sheer magnitude of loss caused the world to pause after the end of WWI in 1918. With 20 million left dead, the major powers of the world stopped to ask *"Why?"* and to contemplate the futility of the Great War. WWII brought with it over 55 million dead and hundreds of millions more wounded or decimated. Cultural reforms throughout the Eastern World killed many more - Mao's "Great Leap Forward" killed 38 million. The Khmer

Rouge, Stalin, radical Islam, radical Christianity, slavery, eugenics, ageism, and the list goes on and on.. All these human tragedies played out because the powers responsible were being run by people who lived deeply within their ego-identified self - whether that be through a personal lens of nationalism, race, religion, or political thought.

The default tendency of a human mind is to shift toward identification with form - meaning that we automatically will associate our culture, religion, or way of life with our sense of self. Along with this, there's a natural tendency for us to view our group as the absolute best group or the "in" group; separate and superior to any outsiders. When a mind is attached to form, and operating deep within the control of the ego, it will criticize, condemn, exclude, and alienate others so as to create a stronger distinction between the perceived other and themselves.

Intelligence in no way protects us from this tendency of the ego to segregate and define ourselves in relation to others. To the contrary, intelligence has historically been used as a means to offer a false legitimacy to the constructs of exclusion. The early twentieth century brought pseudo-sciences such as craniometry (the measuring of skulls to determine intellect), and eugenics. These pseudo-sciences gave scientific power to commonly believed narratives of racism. Additionally, they served to dehumanize and separate those who were different, either ethnically or socially. History is full of examples of highly intelligent people who held racist and limiting views towards people outside of their group.

As technology enables us to embrace autonomy to a greater and greater degree, we are actively becoming separated from our friends, communities, and sense of humanity. Real relationships are reduced to a series of narcissistic posts and likes. "Will Selfie for Likes" has become the unsaid national mantra. Children are growing up in a virtual world full of virtual connections and devoid of the face to face and genuine interactions required to develop mature empathy towards others.

All this technology has created a world in which our minds can constantly be stimulated if we so desire. When our brains are engaged by something external such as music, movies, video games, social media, or twitter, we are moved towards a state of constant ego engagement. According to the Deloitte group, `theaverageAmericanchecstheirFacebookstatus47timesaday.` This means that they are almost constantly seeking validation of an egoic self. The rise of mobile computing and smartphones has allowed us to become constantly engaged and constantly entertained. The effect of this steady stream of diversion has resulted in a world where people are more disconnected from their true spiritual selves than at any other time in human history.

This past weekend I joined a group of friends for a hike in the Rhineland-Pflaz region of Germany. We walked from a small village in Germany over some very respectable hills across the border into France. Our hike was over 30km and took us to eight different castle ruins along the German-French border. It was an extraordinary experience - we took the time to explore each castle along the way and to climb through what remained of their architectural bones. Since it was such a long hike, I took the time to practice some mindful meditative walking between conversations with my friends. I started to think about what life must have been like for the peasants and castle folk during medieval times. Medieval peasants did not have the wealth of diversions we have today. Throughout the vast majority of human history, mankind has mainly lived a life of hard work which was undoubtedly monotonous and difficult by today's standards. Medieval peasants for rarely experienced live music, theatrical performances, or engaged in sports for play. Their diversions were few and far between; special treats in a life of tedium and toil. Peasants were often left alone with their thoughts in quite meditation, engaged in their tedious daily chores. They were living a life of survival, and although it wasn't fun, it was a deliberate and present life. The by-product of this mode of existence is that people did not live so deeply within their own egos. They had a lot of time to spend with themselves, rather than scrambling to avoid themselves through a myriad of extravagant diversions.

So we have reached a new time in history where ego reigns supreme and human values are increasingly being converted to commodities which we collect like meaningless material objects. Quantity of friendships becomes more important than quality and image more important than substance. Humanity is a crossroads.

The ugliness of our past - the death, destruction, subjugation, and upheaval we've seen as a species over the centuries has been the direct result of a lack of connectedness to the true or higher self. When humans operate primarily for the purpose of ego validation they will strive to prove their worth through exclusion, domination, or subjugation. Every evil that we have ever witnessed as a species has been the direct result of the need for humans to support and validate their beliefs connected to a false self.

How Labels Trick Us

The false self loves to identify with labels. The false, or external self, will call itself a Christian, Muslim, Jew, Hindu, Republican, Democrat, Liberal, Progressive, Black, White, Born-Again, Protestant, Intellectual, Poor, Rich, Nationalist… and the list of labels could go on forever. It's ok to hold beliefs but when our identity is defined solely by those beliefs, we are dropping a heavy anchor into the sea of ego and holding tight. Beliefs that serve to define us move us further from our true and higher self. Your true self is an infinite spiritual being that cannot ever be defined by labels. The true self is pure energy. Love and connectedness are hallmarks of the true self. You have the ability to connect with this true self, feel its power and ability to guide and uplift you throughout your entire existence in this Earthly form. Allowing it to direct your thoughts and emotions will manifest anything and everything you desire in this life.

Why Most People are Living for Ego Validation

Simply put, we are entering an age of post humanism. What the hell is post humanism you might ask? This is the state in which humanity finds itself once we have transcended the bounds of our natural existence through the implementation of technology. That may sound confusing at first, but let's look at some examples. Mankind has been around on this planet for roughly the last 200,000 years as accurately as we can tell. The implementation of technology over that time period has accelerated at an exponential rate (I'm using the word exponential in a literal sense, not abstractly). We'll talk more about this exponential growth rate ahead, but for now, let's focus on the fact that for the last 199,970 or so years, we have been without the following:

- Facebook

- Smartphones

- The Internet

- Video games

- Twitter

- Instagram

- Wikipedia

- Netflix

- Tinder

The list goes on and on. You might notice that I'm focusing on the last 30 years or so of human development. The technology prior to that laid the groundwork for the computing revolution. For the most part, technology did not alter human existence in an extreme way until the age of the silicon transistor in personal computers in the mid-1970s. It was at this point that we began to experience an exponential acceleration of computing power which would eventually move us toward a true post human condition.

What does living in a post human era have to do with our happiness and ability to manifest things and people into our lives?

Living in this time means that we are becoming more and more dependent on technology to keep us connected, while at the same time diffusing our social energies in a way that results in a disjointed web of weak social bonds based more on ego validation rather than genuine love and affection for one another.

To be clear, all this technology and ubiquitous forms of communication have also had wonderful benefits. Just today, I chatted via IM with my friend in India, made a business call to Belfast, responded to an email from my mom in Washington DC, and Skyped with my little sister in Los Angeles. I was happy to be able to stay connected to friends and family across the world and would never complain about that. However, humans did not evolve to communicate in this manner. Despite the great benefits technology brings us, it also has the potential to work against us.

All this technology does not automatically equal a dystopia. It's important to note that technology has the ability to liberate us from the confines of oppressive dogma, institutions, governments, or damaging belief systems. Throughout history, we've seen how the dissemination of knowledge leads to a higher collective understanding of the world and how we as humans are meant to interact with each other and the institutions and beliefs that we create as we go along.

The Invention of the Printing Press

In Renaissance Europe, the invention of the printing press in 1440 marked the beginning of massive knowledge redistribution. For the first time in history, knowledge could be shared with the masses relatively cheaply. In less than 100 years, the printing press resulted in the dissolution of the literate elite. Since more people now had access to books, more people began to learn to read. Dissemination of knowledge from the printing of scientific journals resulted in the birth of the scientific revolution which brought technological discoveries at a rapid pace. The protestant reformation, perhaps the most critical event in world history in terms of shaping our modern society, was only possible because Martin Luther's 99 theses and his pamphlets were mass produced on the new printing press. Today, we are seeing similar effects in the political and human-rights spheres with social networking sites such as Facebook. Those living under oppressive and tyrannical governments are able to see how others in free countries live, and they are using social media as a springboard for collective action to change their conditions or bring worldwide attention to their plight.

Your Time Is Now

We are truly living in a time that is unlike any other time period in human history. That means that we will face new problems and those problems will require novel and proven solutions. In this book, I will offer you an ancient strategy, worded to fit our modern age, which will yield you explosive productivity, peace, happiness, and a deep connection with others based on mutual love and respect. By conditioning your mind to operate in a mindful state, you will learn to live within the expression of your true self; free from the restrictions and the misery of the ego. Once you begin operating from the motivations of your true self, you will see happiness and abundance manifest in a miraculous and profound way in your life. You hold in your hands the key to your own happiness and abundance. Everything is up to you. Take the time to embrace your own power to create.

What if I were to tell you that you have the ability to receive anything you ask for from the universe, in a timely and exacting manner, time and time again with predictable results? What if I were to tell you that no matter what your situation right now in life, you have full power and control to turn things around, starting immediately? I hope that your first response is one of true belief and faith. If not, this book will help you to understand how the Law of Attraction is always working to create your reality, whether or not you believe in it, care about it, or even acknowledge its existence. You will learn how to hack into the control mechanisms of this natural force for your immediate and dramatic benefit. Whatever you desire - be it a new car, house, spouse, loyal and honest friends or more money than you will ever need - this can all be yours. The time frame is not important to the universe - in fact, you may likely be shocked at how quickly your desires manifest, when following the secrets within this book.

Using the techniques that you will learn in this book, I have created my dream life. We have the power to change the future and this book will teach you exactly how to do that. Understanding mind bias and the Law of Attraction has enabled me to travel to 51 countries, build friendships across the globe, and live comfortably in Europe with no concerns about money. When you use the Law of Attraction and take action to hack your own mind bias through belief transformation, you will see immediate and life-changing results!

Your success in the areas of love, career, friendship, health, and overall life satisfaction are entirely in your hands. You truly are the creator. Any condition is temporary and can be easily reversed when you apply the principles. Time is of no concern to the universe. I have used the Law of Attraction to radically transform a situation overnight, or in some cases, instantly. The power of belief, coupled with the harnessing of emotional energy, directed toward the manifestation of desire, is an absolutely unstoppable recipe for success. Oftentimes, what seems like a problem now will turn into a blessing of amazing potential. Read and study the pages that follow with laser-like attention. Your future life depends on it.

CHAPTER 2: WHY ARE WE HERE?

On a blustery sunny day in April of 1521, one of the most intelligent yet stubborn monks in history began a ten day trek from his home in Wittenberg, Germany, to the trial of the century. The monk had been called to account for his heretical views and writings against the hypocrisy he saw in the Catholic leadership of the day. The trail against him was scheduled to commence in the far away city of Worms. The monk would most likely be called to the inquisition, tortured, and ultimately burned at the stake. He was anxious about this possibility, but felt an even stronger sense of excitement because he knew this was an opportunity to defend his ideas among the world leaders of the day. He believed so strongly in his ideas, which challenged not only the Catholic Church but also the governments who supported the church at the time that he was willing to give his life in order that the world hear his message. He had already received worrisome news that his life was in danger in his home village of Wittenberg, since the Catholic Church had sent several agents to intercept and kill him. It's with this looming threat of assassination that he gladly left his home town and began the long slow journey toward his final fate in the city of Worms.

As the old monk rode along in a horse cart toward the trial where sure death awaited him, he felt less and less anxious about his fate. He reasoned that as long as he was given the opportunity to confirm and support his positions against the church, he would die content. For him, the truth was the most important thing. The monk's name was Martin Luther, and his resilience, boldness, and commitment to die for the truth, served to change the world for the better. His ideas broke the political and spiritual stranglehold of institutional religion and shook the foundations of the Catholic Church to its core. Martin Luther didn't care about death when the truth was so much more important than his own life. He knew that his ideas about religion and man's existence were soundly and fundamentally true and that they had the potential to help mankind on a massive and unprecedented scale.

As Martin plodded along in the horse cart, he was surprised when large crowds of peasants came out to greet him in every town that he passed through. People brought gifts of food and wine, and offered to let him stay as a guest in their homes. In every village he passed, the people ran out of their homes and greeted him as a liberator. This unexpected popularity among the common people of Germany and their acts of kindness towards him served to further strengthen his resolve. He could see that the masses of oppressed people were hungry for the truth, and ready to receive real knowledge; as well as true freedom from the institutions of the day. He prayed constantly, which he claimed helped him to understand even more fully that his writings against the church were morally just and truthful. His knew that his ideas were worth dying for.

At his trial, he was asked to recant all his previous statements against the church. He refused, and instead gave an elegant and thought-provoking response that left everyone present in awe of his courage. His response was done in a confident and bold manner, and as he stood among the world's elite, he addressed them firmly and directly without fear. Much of his rebuttal was simply irrefutable by anyone because it heavily referenced the foundations of canonical scripture. For example, Martin argued that indulgences, essentially a get out of jail free card that gave the bearer direct entrance to heaven (despite any previous sins they may have committed) was not mentioned anywhere in the bible, and therefore was a man-made creation. He argued that even the idea of indulgences jeopardized the salvation of church members because it offered them a sense of false redemption. God, he argued, would be the only one to provide such redemption.

Despite his amazing response, he was still ultimately condemned as a heretic by church leaders and faced an agonizing death by torture. However, the young prince Frederick the Wise of Saxony granted him twenty-one days to return to his home before being officially declared as a heretic. The young prince then had Martin snatched up on the return trip and taken to a secret castle where Martin was allowed to live out his days in peace, albeit in isolation. Martin continued to write and spread the truth until his dying day.

Why do we read books about improving our lives? Why do we focus so much attention on meeting our own needs and alleviating the suffering we experience? At the root of these questions lies a bigger question: Why are we here and how can we best fulfil our purpose?

I like to think of life as a messy boot camp. When we start life as little children, we are nearly 100% ego. As time passes, we learn through hardship to be more humble. By the time we are ready to die, we've hopefully learned our lessons; we are much less about ego and much more about acceptance and spiritual peace. You've heard that everything happens for a reason. We are infinite spiritual beings. We are not our job, bank account, car, house, or friends. We are not defined by the possessions we own. Our true self exists independent of anything in this world. Our true self is the still small voice inside. It's the intuition that you feel when you're about to make a big decision. It's the detached observer that we notice in a meditation session. It's the pure joy of existence that you feel when you learn to accept yourself with no conditions attached to the physical world of things.

We all have important lessons to learn. That lesson may be as simple as accepting things the way they are. Oddly, it's not until we absolutely learn to accept our current state that the universe starts to give us what we want. Gratitude and experiencing the feelings of "having it now" are part of this acceptance process. These feelings are important, but won't manifest things alone. We must also truly accept things as they are. Right now, at this very moment, everything in your life has occurred for a purpose. Don't be sad because of hardship but instead rejoice because you are in the midst of learning a valuable lesson. It's all part of the messy boot camp which is life, preparing us for something greater beyond our current understanding of the physical realm. As an eternal being, you must grow and learn in order to progress in spirit.

Why are We Here?

I will go ahead and step out on a limb here and say that I think I know why we are here on this Earth. **We are here on this Earth to grow and mature as spiritual beings.** For some of you, that might be a no-brainer. For others, there may be some doubt. Time and time again in life, our egos are tested and beaten down. Time and time again, we are let down, depressed, offended, angered, or jealous because our false self feels threatened. The older we get, the more we realise how little material possessions and money effect our happiness, and how supremely important our relationships are. We realize that the best moments in life occurred when we connected in a real and loving way with others. Our ego is slowly broken down until we can start to see the world from non-judgmental, purely accepting eyes. Our goal is to come back to our true self, and to learn to whole-heartedly love others without comparison or judgement. This is a long process, but recognizing this is what is happening speeds things is up for us.

Later in this book we will examine in depth what I call the "Gift of Adversity". For now, start to understand that you are engaged in an elaborate boot camp of sorts. Boot camps are designed to prepare you for greater things to come. We can't say for sure what that is, but we do know that as eternal beings, this earthly life is just one part of our journey.

You are the Most Precious Thing in the Universe

Ninety-nine percent of the human body is made up of six elements: oxygen, carbon, hydrogen, nitrogen, calcium, and phosphorous. The remaining one percent is made up potassium, Sulphur, chlorine, and magnesium. More than a dozen additional trace elements are present in the human body as well and thought to be required to maintain life. Where do you think all these elements that make up your body, brain, and ultimately your mind come from? They were created deep inside the crushing and extreme heat of stars - the very same stars that you see each night in the sky. Isn't it amazing that the individual elements of which we consist came together to form something as complex and amazing as our bodies? Even more incredible is that the complexity of our brain produces our mind and what we know as individual consciousness.

You are the ultimate expression of the universe; a sentient, intelligent mind capable of pondering your own existence. You've arisen from nothing into something of majestic complexity and beauty. Nowhere else in the universe have we found any signs of life. Within the billions and billions of stars that we have observed, we've found nothing other than hopeful speculation that other forms of life exist. (Check out the rare earth hypothesis or the Fermi Paradox which supports this conclusion)

When you think about the trillions upon trillions of stars in the universe without life, you can start to grasp how incredibly rare and precious each human life really is. Each of us are the ultimate expression of universal energy, and therefore we consist of an aliveness and energy that is unlimited. Every second in time is a precious and beautiful gift. When you understand how precious life is and even more so consciousness, you can truly appreciate your inherent value. The most important time is now, and the most precious thing in the universe is you.

Because you are the universe, you are intrinsically connected to its vast power and beauty. As physicists delve further into the quantum world, they are discovering more evidence that suggest our minds are active participants in the creation process. You are the universe, you are the creator, and you have the power to direct your life as you wish.

From Stardust to Complexity

Why does life in the universe move towards greater and greater levels of complexity? There seems to be an unknown driving force which moves towards basic states of existence into super complex systems. You are the perfect example. You came from the remnants of stars, and ended up over time as the most complex and miraculous machine in the universe - the human body. Beyond complex creatures such as whales and platypuses, it seems that intelligence is the next step in the complexity of life. Intelligence allows us to understand our world and eventually answer all the questions we have about why we are here. When we think honestly about the driving force of nature to create complex systems from seemingly random elements, we must acknowledge that there is some unknown, underlying motivator for this action. You can see this force everything in our world. A tree growing through solid rock, bacteria growing on the bottom of the ocean alongside volcanic heat vents, and many other situations arise in nature where life does its best to survive and thrive at all costs. Life is the expression of a conscious universe saying, "I want to be!" and "I want to experience the world!" All lifeforms are processing data through their senses, and form interpretations of the world around them. Life is the universe's method for experiencing itself.

Moving Past Your Ego Takes Guts

When we think of heroes, we often think of firemen saving babies from a burning building, or a mother donating a kidney to save her son. These people are certainly heroes and exhibit bravery, but in most cases, they are doing what any good person would do given the same situation and training. Not to diminish these sorts of heroic acts in any way, but we should stop to think about bravery and heroism in a different and oftentimes unseen way.

When you confront your own existence, come to terms with your past, galvanize and head toward the future with vision and excitement - you are committing big acts of bravery. Accepting your life for what it is; taking full responsibility for what you have manifested thus far, and taking the steps to look past your ego to what we call the inner or true self - these are the most heroic acts you can commit in your lifetime.

Most people go through life avoiding their own mortality and emotions - jumping from one distraction to the next in order to experience the least amount of pain and suffering. When you recognize this and take the steps to complete the exercises in this book, you will be living a very mindful and deliberate life. Frankly, that takes guts. This takes a level of raw honesty and integrity rarely exhibited by most. Once you complete the exercises in this book, and follow up with the "putting it all together" plan at the end, you will be truly living as you were meant to live. Stripping away the falsehoods that prop up ego and controlling our minds to direct our thought energy, puts us in a position of absolute aliveness and joy. Once in this position, we can direct our lives however we choose, and experience existence in a pure, joyous state of abundance.

Chapter 3: Let's Get Busy!

"In order to carry a positive action we must develop here a positive vision". - *The Dalai Lama*

"Thinking will not overcome fear but action will". - *W. Clement Stone*

As you begin to generate the feelings of having it now, and as you dissolve your limiting beliefs, you will start to receive signs and cues from the universe to *act*. These cues are called **inspired action**. They are hints from the universe that you need to act on. For example, you may have asked the universe for a higher quality and more supportive group of friends with which you share common interests. You might see a poster on a bulletin board that advertises a local club for whatever hobby you are into. This is a cue the universe is sending you. Call the number, meet some new people, and realize that your desire has manifested. Once you start generating the powerful feelings that the Law of Attraction brings, you will soon begin to see all sorts of cues in your life for inspired action. You'll also receive cues when something just isn't right for you. You might have a feeling that a club, event, or a certain person just isn't aligned with the vision you have for your future. In these cases, we need to really listen to these cues for action or inaction. The universe is trying to desperately reach a congruent state between your beliefs and your external reality. It is right 100% of the time. Listen to the cues you receive!

Directed Action

One of my all-time favorite breweries in the United States is Dog Fish Head Brewing Company out of the state of Delaware. Their beers are unique, creative, and delicious. They've taken the most classic of beer styles and Americanized them — highlighting their best features and taking ingredients and innovation to a whole new level. As an avid home brewer, I greatly appreciate the technical skill that's required to produce such masterful beer, but I also admire the tenacity and determination of the brewery's founder for making his dream a reality.

In 1995, Sam Calagione, at the time a poor college student, decided that he wanted to open a brewery and compete with the greatest craft breweries in the world. He dropped out of Columbia, packed up his dorm room, and moved to Delaware with his girlfriend to start building the brewery. Once in Delaware, he raised $220,000 for initial building and operating costs.

Sam ran into a huge obstacle though — in 1995 in Delaware, breweries were actually illegal! The law was a leftover from the prohibition era. A state inspector came down to his build site one day and let him know that he would not be able to proceed with his dream since state law did not allow it.

Sam thought for a minute and stately very simply, *"Well, looks like we're going to have to change the law."* Sam then set about as a one man campaign to lobby the state legislature. The state government was so impressed with his drive and vision for success that they granted his request later that year and retracted the prohibition-era legislation.

By the following year, his little brew pub was packed daily with visitors, and today they see sales of over $50 million a year, distributing all across the United States.

Work in the Moment Only

Directed action is the work that we do every day to achieve our goals. This is a very conscious effort. A good example might be building a small business. You work tirelessly every day to achieve this goal, hoping for a successful business one day. The important thing to understand with directed action is that you must always focus on pursuing excellence in the moment, don't worry about the future. You have already asked the universe to have a business that blows up into a multi-million dollar machine of profit, right? You have already generated a belief that is unwavering regarding this. It will happen! So, don't worry too much about final results long term. There's no mystery here — the future has already been decided. What you must focus your attention on is the task at hand. Moment by moment throughout your day, focus only on pursuing excellence in your actions, words, and thoughts. This means that at each moment, you are doing the absolute very best work that you and your team are capable of. You are working at a world-class optimum level of quality and excellence in that moment. Do this, and you will always be successful.

Fear is Normal

Many times, when you act, you may experience fear. Fear of a new situation, people, or places is normal. It's important not to let this keep you from acting toward your goals. Always approach the action phase of manifestation with a brave and faith filled heart. Be brave. Keep your presence of mind about you and don't let the fear overwhelm you to the point of inaction. For example, if you are starting a new business and leaving an old job you may have security fears. Will I be able to feed my family? Will I lose everything? Prepare for the worst, but expect the best. Recognize and accept the fears, but move forward in your action despite them.

Directed Action with a Plan

We need to act in order to achieve our goals. This is a rather obvious in fact. Most people believe that hard work pays off and it's true it does. However, strong-arming your way toward a goal is both exhausting and time intensive. We should make action plans to achieve goals, but always support our actions with the Law of Attraction. Without faith, actions are meaningless. With faith, actions are powerful and worthy of our efforts. Work smarter, not harder. Make the action plan that you develop for directed action toward a goal efficient and quick. If you need to clean out your garage for example, relying solely on faith will see that manifestation goal achieved much slower than if you combined the faith with directed action. The combination of faith plus action become more important the more complex your desire happens to be.

The Story of the Fisherman

Way down South in Mexico, lived a somewhat lazy fisherman. He spent his days lounging on the beach in the Mexican sun, feeling the cool ocean breezes against his skin, and occasionally catching a fish or two.

One day, an American tourist walked by and witnessed the fisherman pulling in a nice big fish.

"Wow, that's a heck of a fish you have there!" said the American tourist

"Yes it is! This one's a keeper." the Mexican smiled back.

"You know, if you were to open a guide business here on the beach, you could probably save enough money to buy yourself a boat."

The Mexican thought for a moment and then responded, "...And then what?"

"Well, then you could expand your guide business to boat charter trips of course!" Replied the American.

"..And then what"?

The American looked a bit confused, "You could eventually expand your boat charter business into an entire fleet of boats!"

"..And then what?'

"Well, then you could sell your business, retire rich, and spend the rest of your days relaxing on the beach and catching fish, with no cares in the world."

With that, the fisherman closed the lid of his small cooler, popped the top off a beer, reclined in his beach chair and smiled. After a gulp, he said, "Seems like a lot of work for something I already have."

When we put our minds to action toward the pursuit of a goal, **we oftentimes spin our wheels to achieve things that we already have.** Make sure that you're not wasting emotional and physical energy in pursuing things the wrong way. Being in alignment with your true self and the source of all love and power in the universe through a mindful meditative practice will help you to understanding what you are truly seeking, and to find the best path to that goal.

Inspired Action

Inspired action is the action that we take when we are prompted by the universe. These prompts can appear in subtle or explicit ways at any time. You will start to see these prompts from the universe when you are in a state of gratitude and acceptance and also when you are holding extreme faith that a desire will be manifested into your life soon. When you have unwavering faith, the universe attempts to rectify the disparity between the thought energy you are generating and what reality currently is. When you are tuned into the universe, your thought energy will win every time and you will see your desire come into your life.

Remember the story I told you about Sam Calagione and his wildly successful brewery? In interviews as well as his own writings, Sam talks about the time that he understood his destiny and how his brewery got its name. While vacationing with his family in Maine, he and his father took a walk one evening through the local neighborhood. Sam was discussing his dream of opening a brewery when suddenly they both looked up and saw a street sign that seemed to be speaking to them both. The sign said "Dogfish head" and his father causally mentioned that that would make a good name for a brewery. Sam felt something at that moment and knew that his brewery would be called Dogfish Head Brewing Company.

It's important that you stay sensitive to the cues the universe throws your way. You may be prompted to act when your mind is telling you that acting is silly or unnecessary. In these cases, ignore your mind — follow your gut always. You might feel a pull to try a new restaurant, start a new hobby, or call a friend whom you've disconnected with. When we are open and willing to accept that the universe has our best intentions in mind, we will naturally be receptive and sensitive to the sometimes subtle clues it gives us to act. When this happens, it causes us not just to act, but also to be very excited because inspired action results in some of the most miraculous changes in our lives. What otherwise might take years to accomplish with directed brute force action, can occur overnight when inspired action is involved.

One of my best friends has a great story of inspired action and how it can rapidly change your circumstances. My buddy had been married for a little over a year when he landed a new job with a considerable pay raise in another city. This job was essential to his career progression and it would be foolish to turn it down. He and his new bride were excited and began preparing to move from Alabama to New York where the new job was. On the day they were supposed to leave town, my friend could not find his wife anywhere. She wasn't answering her phone, responding to text or social media, and her work had not seen her all day. As that night drew to a close, he became more and more desperate.

Finally, around midnight, he received a call from her mother.

"She doesn't want to be married to you anymore. She's safe but doesn't want to speak with you."

That was the last he heard of his wife. She de-friended him from social media, blocked his phone calls and texts, and instructed her workplace not to take any calls from him. He was devastated to say the least. The next day, he drove to New York hoping that an explanation would be forth coming and that eventually she would come to her senses and join him.

Days stretched into months until one day he received divorce paperwork in the mail. She wanted nothing and all he had to do was sign the forms. With a heavy heart he did so, and dropped them in the mail.

That next weekend, his father was in town visiting him in his new city. As he rode in the car with his father, my friend expressed his deep concern and depression over the inexplicable break up. Alone in a new city and starting a new job, he felt vulnerable, rejected, and overwhelmed with life. As they drove by a church, his father suddenly sat upright in his seat and said, "Son, I think you should go to that church right there tonight."

"Oh ok Dad, thanks…but why"?

"I'm not sure to be honest with you, but I have a strong feeling that something important is waiting there for you." His father, a man of faith, continued, "I have a feeling that all of this will be better if you take this one simple step."

HIs father's words were profoundly received, and he agreed to swing by the church later that night.

That night, in the church parking lot, he met his future wife. They've been happily married now for over 18 years and continue to grow and learn together with their two children. Looking back, he knows now that his life is beyond what he ever would have had if his first wife would *not* have left him. In the midst of his suffering, the universe offered him a doorway to a wonderful life of peace and love through an inspired prompt that his father received. All he had to do was open that door - listen to the cues and take action!

Chapter 4: Emotions: GPS for your Soul

Your emotions are constantly sending you important messages. The degree of emotional turmoil you experience over a problem is directly related to your need to act. Most people don't really accept and claim their own emotions. The girl who stays in a hurtful relationship, the worker who stays at a job with a bad boss due to fear of change, and the alcoholic who refuses to admit he has a problem are all good examples of this. These are all examples of people who are not tuned in and are not being brutally honest with themselves about the messages their emotions are sending. Meditation helps immensely with this because it allows us to fully accept our emotions without judgement against ourselves.

The Psychologist

I recently heard a great story about a psychologist who gave a speech at a mental health conference. Before she was due to speak, she made her way through the crowd and handed out glasses of water for each person. She then came back around with her assistants holding pitchers of water and filled up each glass about half way. Once she was on the stage to give her speech, she briefly introduced herself and then asked the crowd the question, "How heavy is this glass of water that you are holding right now?"

Answers such as "8oz", "12oz", and so forth came from the crowd.

After a pause, the psychologist gave the answer:

She said, "The weight of the water depends on how long you hold the glass."

She continued, "If you hold the glass for one second, it's not very heavy. If you hold the glass for one hour, it gets much heavier. If you hold the glass of water all day, your will experience muscle cramps and aches, and the glass will seem unbearably heavy. So it is with our emotions."

The elegant example the psychologist used in this story describes exactly how our emotions affect us when we refuse to experience them fully. Many times painful emotions are avoided to the extent that we suppress them or use what I call "dangerous diversions" to redirect them. You'll learn more about dangerous diversions later in this book. They can include drug and alcohol use as well as any means we find to avoid reality. We find that the best way to deal with emotions is oftentimes counterintuitive to where our brain's self-preservation mechanisms take us. For example, a depressed individual may need to be with supportive friends and family in order to heal, but the mind will lead a depressed person to self-isolate as a protective mechanism. This will lead to an even worse depression.

Our Mind Doesn't Always Know Best

In the winters, I teach ski lessons for the local Army morale and welfare branch at a nearby US military installation. When I teach total beginners to ski, I am fighting against their natural self-preservation instincts. For example, typically when a beginner skier starts to build up some speed as they are going downhill, their brain immediately goes into self-preservation mode and wants them to slow down. They do this by instinctively sitting back on their skis. It almost looks like they are riding a motorcycle. The effect this has is to only engage the rear part of their skis, thereby giving them *less* overall control. The correct form is actually to lean slightly forward, with their shins pushing gently into the front of their ski boots. This has the effect of engaging the entire length of the ski which will then enable them to turn or stop with total control. The action of leaning slightly forward feels completely counterintuitive to what their brains are telling them to do. They must un-learn their natural self-preservation instincts in order to gain greater control.

So too is it the same with our emotional health! In order to be fully in control, mindfully present and happy, we must *not* avoid negative emotions. To the contrary, we must lean into them if you will, and allow ourselves to fully experience the pain.

Emotions as Response to Crisis

There is another type of emotional pain that doesn't have anything to do with ego validation and that is simply due to situations that might arise in our lives. The death of a loved one for example can cause enormous suffering. Perhaps you've experience loss in the way of a divorce, cheating, dishonest friends, or any number of less than ideal situations in life. Oftentimes we stuff these down and suppress the ugly emotions these situations generate for years and years. This will lead to all sorts of latent physical and emotional issues. Only by acknowledging your emotions immediately and allowing yourself to fully experience the pain can you move forward in a healthy way.

Easier Said than Done

When you are feeling down, discouraged, angry, or hurt in any way, advice such as "pull yourself out of it", "be grateful for what you have.", or "try to see the positive side.." all seem to fall short in providing us much in the way of relief. There are ways that we can bootstrap ourselves out of an emotional black hole. Many years ago, I developed a technique to process painful emotions. I call it the Green Blob Method.

The Green Blob Method

I've found a very simple and highly effective technique that I call the "Green Blob Method" which allows me to fully experience the negative emotion, dissolve its power to cause lingering suffering, and provides immediate relief. Here's how it works:

Externalize - Think of the negative emotion as something completely external to yourself. Imagine it as a blob of green energy floating outside of your body. This green blob wants to connect to your false self. It represents pain to the ego and hence the ego tries to avoid it at all costs. Picture a complete and fully formed physical green blob in the room with you. It helps to think back to the original ghostbusters movie. This could even make you start laughing!

Feel - Feel the emotion fully - do not turn away from it. Allow yourself to deeply experience any discomfort and pain that the emotion brings. If you need to cry go ahead. No one will judge you as weak for crying. Whatever pain surfaces, let it arise naturally. Do not try to suppress any part of it. You are being entirely honest with yourself and allowing yourself to feel exactly how you should feel at this time. As you are experiencing all that the emotion brings to surface, continue to visualize it as something external to you — a big green blob floating in the room. The emotion isn't you — you are simply observing the emotion.

Process - Continue to process the emotion as an EXTERNAL entity. Although you are fully experiencing the green blob of emotion, know that this is NOT you. This emotion has nothing to do with your identify or sense of self. It is simply an external object that is part of your experience as a human being. You are not rejecting it, but simply accepting it peacefully.

Connect - Realize the emotion cannot alter or touch your true self in any way. Your true self is impervious to this external green blob of emotion. The green blob of emotional pain has no arms or legs. It's really a soft gelatinous blob of harmless emotional energy that can't hurt you. You are safe. Your true self is infinite and untouchable. Only your ego is affected by the green blob because your ego also exists as an external entity. Your true self can never be harmed by painful emotions.

I share this four stage technique with you early on so that you can start right now to shift your emotional energy toward an abundant state. As you'll learn later, emotions are extremely important to effectively and quickly manifest our desires. If you can start right now to accept your latent negative emotions, process them so as to diffuse and disarm their ability to thwart you physically, mentally, and spiritually; you will be in a much better position to start manifesting anything and everything you've ever dreamed of in your life. Don't allow the weight and burden of a green blob of negative emotion to hold you back. Follow the above process and you will free yourself from its shackles. Depending on the size of your green blob, you may have to run through the process multiple times until the emotions are completely processed and diffused.

Fostering Positive Emotions

One of the key catch phrases you'll hear when studying the Law of Attraction are the words "Like attracts like". We should definitely keep this in mind when we are processing about our emotions. When you are happy, joyful, and excited for your current circumstances, you will attract more positive emotions and circumstances into your life. You will continue to feel more and more confident, fulfilled, and at peace with your life as you progress in your practice of mindfulness and deliberate living. Thus, you should avoid negative places, people, events, movies, and news in order to avoid bringing negative emotions into your experience. Sometimes these things can't be avoided, such as in the case of certain professions like the military, police officers, and emergency room personnel. You cannot shield yourself completely from sad or negative events and emotions; especially in careers such as these. Luckily for us, there's an easy and effective way to counteract these negative emotions. We can do things that make us laugh and take life less seriously.

The Most Important Lesson I Learned from a Friend

A good buddy of mine lived with me for a few months as he was transitioning between houses. Every day, he would watch the goofy cartoon series, Family Guy, on Netflix. He would binge watch this show and at first it was a little annoying as I never really much cared for it. I was more in the habit of watching documentaries about various military conflicts throughout history as well as other darker subjects at the time such as the holocaust and other atrocities. I tolerated him watching the show and just did my writing and painting in the background. After a week or so, I was laughing along with all the stupid jokes. I watched so many episodes of the family guy that I started to take life in general less seriously. The silly comedy from the show spilled over into my general thinking and I began to laugh at things that normally would have annoyed me. I noticed that anytime I was watching something serious, my friend would ask if we could watch something less depressing. I complied, and we would watch more Family Guy episodes. As I continually put myself into states of laughter, I noticed that I was experiencing more laughter and fun at work too. Generating states of laughter and fun will attract more of the same, and you will find that life, taken less seriously, is a lot easier overall.

Our Evolution Causes us to Obsess Over Negative Things

It's a natural tendency of the human mind to want to obsess over negative or dark subjects. It's built into our evolution. Our minds want to constantly analyze our environment as well as the people we associate with in order to identity potential threats to our safety. This means that our brains are wired to filter data with a negative bias. This is why we sometimes become fascinated by dark material; political shows that lambast and demonize the other side, documentaries about evil dictators, the holocaust, and the horrors of trench warfare are some examples. Horror movies, Halloween, the Mexican Day of the dead, and Stephen King novels all tap into this tendency of our mind to obsess over dark subjects. From an evolutionary perspective it makes sense - it was safer for us to immediately distrust others and assume the worst rather than the opposite. Additionally, we would want to view all incoming info as potentially dangerous before deciding that it was in fact safe.

This bias toward negative thinking has served to protect us throughout time. However, we no longer have to worry about strangers clubbing us to death to steal our food supply. Our homes are not likely to be raided by bandits, and most likely you will not have to run from a sabre tooth tiger in order to reach work safely each day. Although our tendency to think negatively still protects us from danger, we are living in a world where this evolutionary trait is more outdated and cumbersome than helpful. Thus, we must work to overcome this bias toward negative thinking, and continually put ourselves in a state of happiness and relaxation.

An easy way to overcome this innate bias is to actively recognize your thoughts without fully accepting them as fact. This means that you will start to notice a little delay between the thought and the *processing* of that thought as truth. For example, you might immediately assume the worst about someone; you might assume that a person is lying when they say "something came up" and they are unable to attend your party. Instead of accepting this thought immediately as fact, first recognize the thought itself. In other words, simply say to yourself, "I just had the thought that so and so was being dishonest with me."

Recognizing that the thought is simply a thought and not a fact will enable you to identify what is factual and what is your innate bias toward negative thinking. If you have no reason to believe that your friend is lying, then you should accept them at their word and assume the best. This will generate feelings of compassion, trust, and acceptance rather than resentment and mistrust. It's always better to assume the best and move on unless given objective evidence to the contrary. Simply relying on your own thinking might cause you to assume the worst. When we assume the worst, negative feelings follow and since "like attracts like", your negative assumptions will most likely manifest negative circumstances.

Later we will cover mind bias in an entire chapter but this is a first glimpse of what we need to understand in order to be able to effectively engage the power of the Law of Attraction and mindfulness. The above process of recognizing a thought as a thought first and not a fact is called mindful thinking. Mindful thinking means that we separate the activity of our mind from our concept of self. Our thoughts and feelings are not us - they are merely mental activity and do not define our pure essence and identity as eternal, spiritual beings.

EXERCISE 1

On a sheet of blank paper, write out the top three negative emotions that you are currently experiencing. It might be fear of failure, worries over your children or other family members, or anything else that is consistently bothering you and generating negative energy.

Take each emotion, use the green blob method and allow yourself to fully experience each one. Crying is allowed here. As you fully experience the emotion, you are also diminishing its power and releasing it from your mind. Repeat the green blob method several times for each emotion until you are no longer suppressing any negative emotions. Once you feel the effects of the emotion leave your body, you will feel as though a heavy weight has been lifted off of you. Many people tell me they actually feel physically lighter after using this technique. In this cathartic state, proceed to the next chapter. Repeat this process any time you feel negative emotions.

CHAPTER 5: THE BIG YOU AND THE LITTLE YOU

You become the victim of your own perceptions. Perceptions, arising out of our beliefs, form biased thoughts that activate needless pain and suffering. To escape this, we must strive to process reality accurately and free from the damaging effects of negativity. Additionally, and probably even more importantly, we must learn acceptance of what is, without judgement or comparison.

This mindset, to the person who has never practiced mindful meditation, may sound foreign and confusing at first. After reading this chapter, you will understand better what I'm describing here, and how developing a practice of daily meditation can help you to achieve a level of happiness and satisfaction that you never dreamed possible.

Before we jump into the whys and hows of why mindful meditation works, you need to understand that there are actually two yous. Yep, that's correct - there are really two of you in that big brain of yours - what we call the little you and the big you.

The big you is the *you* that you are probably most familiar with - it's the part of you that craves success, new cars, jewelry, and Rolex watches. This is the *you* that is seeking happiness through the collection of material goods and needs external validation through the admiration of others.

I can recall a very humorous conversation with a good friend of mine last summer as we sat at an outdoor cafe in Budapest. I felt comfortable and close enough to be very direct with this friend as we have known each other a long time. I noticed that he was wearing a very expensive Movado watch. Knowing that he did not make an exorbitant income, I asked him why he would make such an expensive purpose. Here's a breakdown of the conversation:

"Wow, nice watch man! Did you buy that?"

"Yes, I really like Movados"

"Why are they so expensive? Does it do anything besides tell time?"

"No - it just tells the time"

"Oh. Then why did you spend thousands of dollars on it? Wouldn't a regular watch work the same?"

"Um.. I just like it."

"So did you buy it to impress others?"

"No! (a bit angry), I just like it."

"So you're saying that you didn't buy it to impress others, and that it doesn't provide any special functions that would justify you spending about a fifth of your yearly income on it. Can you see how that doesn't seem logical?"

"Yes...(after a long pause) ...ok I suppose I bought it to impress people."

"So, if the watch serves the purpose for which you bought it and attracts others due to their incorrect perception that you are rich, will they like you because they think you are rich or because they legitimately find you interesting and worthwhile?"

"They'll be attracted to me because they think I'm rich."

"You're a pretty amazing person - and people will like you for who you are as a person - not for some egocentric front."

"Ok, valid point. Cheers."

Money Doesn't Buy Happiness, But...

The words, "money doesn't buy happiness" is cliché, but like most clichés, it rings true for the most part. Studies show that in the developed world, money *does* buy happiness to about $50,000 a year because it is at this level that all our basic needs are met and we can engage in most of the leisure activities that we desire. Beyond that amount, additional income doesn't really offer additional happiness. There's not a linear relationship. This doesn't stop people from jumping on the hamster wheel of consumption and working their fingers to the bone in order to earn more money. Don't waste your life to achieve riches and neglect the important things in life such as your relationships with friends and family. Happiness is found in relationships and self-acceptance, not in things.

So, back to the big you, aka the ego. We need the big you in order to function to a certain extent. However, happiness and discontent come knocking when the big you takes control and dominates our thinking. For the majority of the world, the big you is totally in control. The big you loves to compare, contrast, criticize, condemn, complain and exclude others. This is the part of you that wants to be better than your neighbor; wants to be admired and followed. The big you needs to be fed with houses, beautiful mates, narcissistic and shallow friendships, motorcycles, boats, and the list goes on and on. There's nothing wrong with wanting toys as long as the desire is for the functionally fun value they provide. By the way, "functionally fun" is not an oxymoron. If you own a motorcycle, and you love the way it feels to ride and it brings excitement into your life, then it provides a functional recreation service to you. On the other hand, if you desire a motorcycle simply to impress other people, your motivations for owning it are arising from the desire for external validation of your self-worth. When we do things like this, it puts our self-worth in the hands of other people, which is where it shouldn't be. (Don't interpret this to mean that you should sell all your possessions and wear trash bags for clothes. Owning things is perfectly ok - but what we should be conscious of is our internal motivations for owning things).

You might ask - "Why is operating with the big you in control so bad?" This is a legitimate question. The big you can never be satisfied. Once one goal is achieved, another goal replaces that one and you start to work toward obtaining something else that the big you desires. The terms "starter house" and "starter marriage" arise from the never-ending dissatisfaction that the big you inevitably brings. Warren Buffet is today worth an estimated $68,000,000,000 US. (I chose to write the zeros instead of the word "billions" for more impact) Warren still lives in the same house that he purchased way back in 1958 for $31,500. Occasionally someone will interview him and ask why he has not upgraded to a mega-mansion or two. His responses clearly show that he understands the limitations of material possessions to provide happiness. He recognizes the "functionally fun" factor while at the same time having a strong understanding behind his own motivations for ownership:

"Some material things make my life more enjoyable; many, however, would not. I like having an expensive private plane, but owning

a half-dozen homes would be a burden. Too often, a vast collection of possessions ends up possessing its owner. The asset I most value, aside from health, is interesting, diverse, and long-standing friends".
- Warren Buffett

Connecting with Your True Self

When we start to connect with the little you and allow it to guide our motivations and actions, we find that we start to value more important things. Capitalism doesn't necessarily want everyone living within the control of the little you, because much of the rampant capitalism we experience today depends on the desires of the big you seeking external validation through possession collection. **The desires of the little you are oftentimes intangibles that cannot be bought or sold.** Love, friendship, loyalty, laughter, health, peace, and happiness are all things that the little you seeks.

So the term, "little you" is a bit misleading because the inner self is not actually smaller than and compartmentalized from, the big you. In fact, the little you contains the entirety of your consciousness including the big you, the little you, and all of the unconscious aspects of your mind that make up who you are. Some people refer to the little you as the *higher self*, the *inner self*, or the *spiritual self*. I'm going to call the little you the **true self** from this point forward. I like to refer to the little you as your "true" self because it implies that the big you is false, and more accurately describes you as a spiritual and eternal being.

What do you think happens when you meditate and fully clear your mind? You are left alone with nothingness; no thoughts, no objects to cling to, no emotions or beliefs to ramp up your thoughts. If you can work to maintain a state of not thinking for a while, you'll start to feel the natural emergence of your true self. It will take longer for some people to find it, but you will always know when it starts to emerge. Connecting with your true self is infinite, eternal, divine, and beautiful. Those who initially doubt its existence will know once they've experienced it. Each time you are able to touch your true self in meditation, you pull away some of its divine energy. This energy will permeate your entire life and transform your thinking in truly wonderful ways.

Practicing Mindful Meditation

If you've never practiced mindful meditation before and don't know where to start - never fear - I'm going to give you a step by step procedure in chapter 6 to get you started, along with exercises you can do to help generate a mindful state throughout the day. We can practice mindfulness in everything we do: exercising, cleaning, walking, a conversation with a friend, or even during sex. Bringing mindfulness into your life is the single best thing you can ever do for your mental well-being and spiritual health.

The Power of Connecting with Your True Self

When we meditate, we have the ability to go deep into our consciousness and touch base with our true self, drawing upon its eternal and limitless nature. Doing this allows us to understand the big you - the sense of identity we define by external things and opinions. Learning to connect to your true self allows you to turn the volume down on the rest of the world. Suddenly, things aren't so important to us and we operate with an inherent peace and happiness which is persistent; independent of our external reality and circumstances.

It takes some time and practice, but the more time we spend in meditation getting to know our true self, the less vulnerable we will be to the ups and downs of the world around us. We have the ability to become impervious to insults, put-downs, and narcissistic individuals. Additionally, we will no longer require constant praise, companionship, paper friends, and a ton of Facebook likes in order to support a positive sense of self. This freedom and self-assuredness allows us to see through the thick film of egoism in others, as well as identify egoistic behaviors in ourselves. Our relationships become real, genuine, mutually beneficial, and above all - honest.

People who learn to connect to their true self operate with compassion, love, and understanding. They aren't afraid to speak their opinions, even if that means they hold a contrary view to the group; since their self-worth isn't defined by group think or individual opinions. They develop a resilience to the world that is not a Band-Aid but rather a genuine independence that survives adversity. When you don't need people or things to support your sense of worth, you can bravely and passionately pursue your desires. Change comes from the inside out and can only start when we are able to identify the big you and the little you which is your true self.

Chapter 6: Understanding Mind Bias

"What we are today comes from our thoughts of yesterday, and our present thoughts build our life of tomorrow: Our life is the creation of our mind." -The Buddha

"Keep your thoughts positive, because your thoughts become your words. Keep your words positive, because your words become your behaviors. Keep your behaviors positive, because your behaviours become your habits. Keep your habits positive, because your habits become your values. Keep your values positive, because your values become your destiny." - Ghandi

A Story of Two Explorers

Towards the end of the year 1911, two men set off on a journey never before attempted in world history. Robert Scott, a British naval captain, and Roald Amundsen, a Norwegian born explorer, began two separate and distinct journeys with the same goal that ended vastly different ways. Both men took a crew and set off by ship from Europe with the same objective - to be the first man to stand at the South Pole of the globe. Both men planned their expeditions for years in advance, and both men had extensive experience in extreme environments. Both men's expeditions began within a few months of one another and both had a similar tonnage of supplies. Both parties benefited from identical technology and both parties consisted of five man teams. Despite their commonalities, there was one key difference between the two expeditions that proved to be the foundation of success for one, and death for the other.

Amundsen was an adventurer by heart. As a boy, he watched his three older brothers grow up to join the family shipping business just as their father and grandfather had. His mother wanted more from him and pushed him to study hard and become a medical doctor. Each night before bed, young Roald would read about the great explorers in Greenland and other new and exciting places being explored in the world. The stories of the day painted these expeditions as intense but heroic efforts punctuated by periods of fun and playfulness.

To respect his mother, he did as she wished and studied diligently, all the while dreaming of a life on the open seas, exploring new lands. His academic efforts paid off and he was admitted to medical school and was on track to become a physician until his mother suddenly died when he was 21 years of age. With her death, he felt that he no longer had to honour her wish for him to become a medical doctor and he committed himself to following his true passion. Roald promptly dropped out of medical school and enlisted in the Belgian Arctic expedition of 1897. This expedition launched a wildly successful career as a world famous adventurer and explorer.

In contrast, Robert Scott's approach to the Antarctic expedition of 1912 was grounded more out of necessity and the pursuit of scientific research rather than as a fun fast, adventure as Amundsen envisaged. As a result, Scott made decisions about his expedition that were in line with his view of how expeditions should be. Robert Scott was in financial turmoil at the time of the 1912 expedition, and he felt obliged to deliver scientific results to his backers. His family had just sold their lucrative brewery and made some very poor investments which had resulted in bankruptcy. Amid these setbacks, two of Robert's brothers also passed away due to illness which left the remaining family to rely solely on the income that Scott was able to provide. With these pressures, he set off for the Antarctic with the mindset that the expedition was going to be hard, arduous work, and that the whole thing was a necessary pursuit for his family's financial survival.

When you study the two expeditions, you can start to see how mind bias works to affect our every decision. We make decisions based on how we believe things should be. Robert Scott chose to move his supplies with the use of ponies and man-hauling. Man-hauling was laborious and burned too many calories to be a sustainable method of transport in the Antarctic. Amundsen on the other hand, chose to use dogs and skis and go as fast as possible in order to avoid fatigue and to reach their goal quickly. Amundsen knew how critical the overall weight of supplies would be and he understood how important maintaining his men's energy was to their success. As a result, he factored in the deaths of several of his dogs as an unavoidable side effect of the journey. He used the death of the dogs to his advantage, and he actually planned for the men to eat them on the return journey. Using the dogs for food enabled him to travel lighter, and provided extra calories for his men. All in all, Amundsen was quick, light, and smart in his approach to the South Pole. His plan was simple and effective. Amundsen loved to ski and as a result he outfitted his men with super-fast skis of the lightest wood available at the time. His tactics matched the emotions and beliefs he held about exploration. He viewed exploring as an adventure, full of wonder and excitement.

Scott viewed exploration as a job; arduous and unrelenting. He believed that exploration wasn't meant to be fun and exciting. He approached his mission to the South Pole with total scientific reasoning and scrutiny. Scott felt that exploration of this nature was an inherent struggle, and that real scientific progress only came with hard work and sacrifice. The decisions he made in the planning stages served his team poorly in the end. Scott paused throughout the journey to conduct experiments, and relied primarily on man-hauling, the manual pulling of heavy sleds loaded with supplies, to move his camp. His plans were overly complex, which did not allow for anything to go wrong. When his party ran out of supplies, the men suggested that they eat the ponies, but Scott refused on the grounds that it wasn't dignified and wasn't part of their plan. His inability to turn a bad situation into something good made their situation worse. Instead of skis, Scott's men were made to walk, adding to their exhaustion and slowing the entire team down.

When Scott's men finally reached the South Pole on January 17th, 1912, they found a note from Amundsen waiting for them. He had reached the pole 34 days prior. Scott's men started the trek back with down trodden hearts. Day by day, their situation worsened. On February 17th, the first man died. By March, Scott and all of his men were dead. Their final encampment was just 18km from a large depot of supplies that would have saved their lives. News of the tragedy did not reach the rest of the world until more than a year later. A country mourned their loss and the world acknowledged their sacrifice made in the pursuit of science.

Roald Amundsen, the fun-loving Norwegian explorer, completed his journey round trip in 99 days and did not lose a single man. He returned to Europe a hero and the world rejoiced at his accomplishment. Amundsen went on to become a national hero, exploring many other remote places on the globe. He left a legacy of adventure, passion, and excitement that still lives on to this day.

How Our Brains Construct Reality

Our brains are extraordinarily interesting things. Its main goal in life is to decode the sensory inputs it receives, and to then construct some logical meaning and purpose from those inputs. The brain uses all available data to construct a sensible, believable world in which we can function and live our lives.

With our five sensory inputs of touch, sight, sound, smell, and taste, our brains create an elaborate reality of incredible complexity. This creation occurs through sense processing and is deceptively illusory in nature. The "real" world consists purely of information and nothing more. Our brain takes this information and makes something useful of it. The major problem with this process is that sensory processing results in a world that is far from real. Due to missing information, the brain has a tendency to "fill in the gaps" so as to provide your mind with a sensible, fluid, and meaningful reality.

We see this most apparently with blind people. Without the sensory input of sight, the brain constructs a reality based on the information it has available. For the blind, physical objects and colors become associated with the senses of touch and sound. The brain of a blind person learns to fill in the gaps and form a conceptual understanding of the external world. The mind always works to provide meaning and purpose and if insufficient data is present for it to do so, it will make inferences based on available data and held beliefs about the world.

Two Realities

Of great significance is the fact that we are dealing with two realities - the reality of the outside world and the reality that our mind constructs. The reality of the outside world is simply data. Our senses are essentially data collectors that send information to the brain for processing. The brain then constructs a perceived reality from the aggregate sense information. Surprisingly, the outside reality does not consist of lots and lots of data. Rather, our brains are left to piece together meaning from very limited information. The reality that we experience is fully constructed in the brain. The appearance of a smooth, consistent, and external reality is merely a very good illusion which our brain generates in order to provide us a sense of completeness and consistency. The famous philosopher Bertrand Russell first addressed this in his classic, "Problems of Philosophy" in which he coined the term "sense-data".

How Beliefs Guide our Perception

Many times when our brain has to fill in the gaps it results in a useful and harmless outcome. However, when presented with larger more complex problems or when the brain has less data to work with, the brain must then fall back to one of its most powerful mechanisms of sensory perception: belief.

Beliefs are core ideas about the world, yourself, other people. Beliefs include ideas we hold about entire social or ethnic groups and reality in general. Racism is a poignant example of this. People are taught through overt and sometimes subtle propaganda that a certain race has undesirable qualities. This results in the masses developing a core belief about that race that colors their perceptions. Once this belief is grounded, whenever the racist individual encounters someone from that ethnic group, they immediately presume certain things about them. A friendly gesture can be perceived wrongly as a threat. A smile can be perceived as a grimace. Any action can be wrongly perceived as confrontational and aggressive. The *belief* has caused the mind to construct a world that doesn't match reality.

The brain always relies on beliefs when it has to make a decision based on limited information. With insufficient data, the brain is oftentimes at a crossroads. This happens very often in social situations. Let's say for instance that you are driving on a congested, busy road and a driver cuts you off. The driver raises his hand and waves in an attempt to apologize. You may however, misinterpret the wave as an offensive rebuke and immediately respond by giving him the bird. In this case, your brain constructed a perception based on limited data. In this process, it used a belief along the lines of, "All drivers who cut me off are assholes". When your brain sees the apologetic driver raise their hand to wave, you immediately process the information through this filter of belief. We call this "mind bias".

Beliefs exist between the data of the outside reality, and the constructed reality of the mind. Beliefs result in a mind bias that colors all our perceptions. An easy analogy to this would be if you were to put on some rose colored glasses. The glasses alter your sensory perception of sight so that you view everything around you with a pink patina. The glasses are serving as a filter which alters your sense perception. In this same way, beliefs alter our more complex sense perceptions and the larger judgments that we make about our world.

The Role of Beliefs in Politics

A good example of how beliefs alter our larger perceptions can be seen in politics. Let's say that you are strongly ideologically opposed to a particular political party. When watching a debate or speech from a member of this political party, you may find it difficult to listen and make judgements about his or her actions in an objective manner. If you hold the belief, "all Republicans are stupid" for example, you will find that you process the person's words through this filter. The result is that you likely are not forming an entirely accurate conclusion but are rather "filling in the gaps" using your mind bias.

The Ultimate Rule When Dealing with Others

When you automatically give people the benefit of the doubt, and always assume friendly intent, you will almost always manifest positive, friendly, and supportive people into your life. Even when someone slights you or attempts to insult you, **always assume positive intent**. Perhaps someone felt close enough to you to be able to have a friendly jab at you, or they may have had something going on in their life that caused them to behave in a negative way. When you reframe their actions in your mind, you create positive and friendly energy. People treat you exactly how you expect them to treat you. Instead of feeling slighted by a perceived insult, be thankful that that person felt close enough to you to poke fun.

Chronically negative and narcissistic types have their own story and it's *not* your story. Later in this book we'll learn how to identify these types of people, but always remember that their story is not yours, and you will continue to live your life in a positive and meaningful way regardless of their negative behavior.

We have a tendency to dwell on the negative when it comes to others. *Why didn't so and so call me back or respond to my party invite? Why didn't she like my post on Facebook? Why wasn't I invited to the party?* When we dwell and ruminate on these things, it creates negative energy that will manifest future negative situations. Instead of ruminating on how you were slighted, assume that there's a valid reason for their behavior, and that the person sees you in high regard and has positive and friendly intent. Don't waste a minute assuming anything other than positive intent!

Creating the mind bias of positive intent when dealing with people is hard to do. It's really not a natural tendency for us due to the bias that evolution has saddled us with.

As stated previously, we've evolved to be naturally suspicious of others. Viewed through the lens of evolution this has served us well to protect us from potential enemies that could threaten our survival. This tendency can also lead us to falsely assume that someone has ill intent. In most cases, people aren't spending much if any time thinking about you at all. When they are thinking about you, it's usually in a positive or neutral way. Until a person gives you sufficient evidence to make you believe they have ill-will toward you, always assume that their intent is positive.

Even after you've identified that a person is blatantly negative towards you, their condition is most likely a temporary one. You have the ability to change someone's perception of you instantly with every interaction you have with them. If you start with the belief that the other person is your friend, they will normally match the belief you hold about them.

Our Flawed Perceptions Make Us Vulnerable

Although our perceptions to us *feel* accurate, psychologists and neuroscientists have identified filter systems that reveal that our perceptions are almost always skewed. Our conclusions about reality are based on what the brain pieces together from limited bits of information. The brain uses internal algorithms to determine what most likely is really happening around us. For example, when you look at the sky in the middle of the day, they brain expects to see the colour blue. Given any sense of ambiguity, the brain will draw the conclusion that the sky is blue, even though it might not be in that particular instant. The danger with these filter systems, or 'cognitive biases' is that they are operating in the background without our knowledge.

Scientists have identified at least twenty different examples of what they call cognitive biases which cause us to oftentimes draw the wrong conclusions. Awareness of these innate biases are important because they are constantly being used against us in marketing, advertising, business negotiations, and even in your social groups. Most cognitive biases are products of our evolution and just run in the background, forever distorting our perceptions. The good news is that we have the ability to become aware of these innate biases and include that awareness in our everyday thinking so as to develop a more accurate understanding of the world and others. Listed below are some of the cognitive biases thus identified:

Anchoring Bias

We tend to hold on or anchor to the first piece of information we hear. For example, if we are told that someone is a bad person through gossip and we have no other information about that person, we will tend to view that person as bad even though we may later discover information which contradicts this belief. Another example is during salary negotiations - the first person to offer a reasonable salary tends to set the acceptable range for negotiation. The first piece of information is automatically used as a reference point from which all other pieces of information are relative.

Availability Heuristic

We tend to place a higher value on information which is directly available to us. For example, someone living in the United States may have been told that the US dollar is the "gold standard" of worldwide currency. From this available information, they may draw the incorrect conclusion that they can use cash dollars in most countries. I have a friend from the states who drew this conclusion and brought $500 US with him when he flew to visit me in Germany. Even though I told him that he would not be able to spend his US dollars anywhere in the EU, he brought them anyway because his bias toward the information available to him was so strong that he was unable to overcome his set belief. Needless to say, he left Europe 10 days later with $500 in his wallet.

Bandwagon Effect

We tend to think that a piece of information is more correct based on the number of people who hold that belief to be true. History is full of examples. For most of modern human history, everyone in the entire world thought that the earth was flat. All the way back to the 3rd century BC, a few thoughtful astronomers said that the Earth was round. Throughout the centuries, more and more experts concluded that the Earth was in fact round, However, it wasn't until 1522 when Magellan completed his voyage around the world that the general populous agreed with the idea of a round Earth. Up until the nineteenth century, there were people who refused to believe it, and clung to the idea of a flat Earth. From the first time the idea of a round Earth was presented by astronomers, it took approximately 1,700 years for the majority of the Earth's population to believe that the Earth was actually round. The bandwagon effect can cause us to cling to ignorance, but it can also lead us to form dangerous conclusions. We can see the dangers of the bandwagon effect in areas such as politics, global warming debates, GMOs, and tobacco use.

Blind Spot Bias

We tend to see the biases in others but not ourselves. An obvious example is the extreme polarisation which we see in American politics. Republicans and democrats love to point out the inherent biases of the other side yet see nothing wrong with their own biased thinking. Night after night, viewers tune in to Fox News or MSNBC, and watch shows which are built around highlighting the biases of their political opponents. Fox news will talk about how the liberals are too blinded by idealism to form accurate perceptions of the current political situation while claiming to have a purely objective and unbiased approach themselves. On the flip side, networks such as MSNBC will present information which suggests conservatives are blinded by rigid dogma, and will do so with an air of humble objectivity. In reality, both sides are suffering the effects of blind spot bias.

Choice Supportive Bias

We tend to think that the choices we make are correct, even when presented with evidence to the contrary. We want to think that our minds are highly capable of coming to accurate conclusions. We want to think that the decisions we make are always valid and based on logical and objective reasoning. The mind has such a need to view its constructed perceptions as accurate that it assumes very high validity when it comes to the decisions we make. The problem with this occurs when we happen to make a bad decision, and we hold onto that decision, regardless of the negative outcomes. My girlfriend recently fell prey to choice supportive bias when she decided to pet a wild raccoon in the Canadian wilderness. Upon seeing a raccoon during the day in a national park where she was camping, she approached it cautiously with some food in hand. The raccoon didn't hesitate to reach up and scratch her hand, snatching the food away in the process. The scratch drew blood, and her best friend, who is a medical doctor, advised her that she needed to go to the hospital for a rabies vaccination. After dressing her wound and googling the potential dangers of being scratched by a wild raccoon, my girlfriend made the decision that she was fine and that she was not going to go to the hospital. When I got word of this, I also advised her to get the vaccine. She firmly refused and stated, "I've made my decision!" Even though she was presented with evidence that her decision wasn't the best course of action, she chose to stand by it because her bias was acting to tell her that her decision was more valid than the opinions of others. (So far thankfully she's showed no signs of rabies!).

Clustering Illusion

We tend to place meaning on clusters of random events. The clustering illusion is a side effect of the mind attempting to predict the future based on the observation of past events. The most glaring example of this occurs with gambler's fallacy. This is the incorrect belief that if someone flips a coin and comes up heads ten times in a row, they are more likely to come up heads on the eleventh flip. Although the probability of eleven heads in a row is extremely low, the probability of ten heads and one tail has the same low probability. So the actual chance of a player hitting heads is still 1/2. Smart gamblers understand a concept called 'base probability' which is the probability of an event occurring *without* considering past events. Casinos across the world rely on the clustering illusion bias to generate enormous income. Next time you gamble, consider the base probability of your given game. In other words, ignore how many times the roulette wheel has hit red. Your wallet will thank you for it!

Confirmation bias

We tend to only seek out process that information which confirms our already held beliefs. This is similar to choice supportive bias in that the brain wants to believe that its strongly held beliefs are the result of reasonable and accurate logic. So what we tend to do is look for sources of information that only support the beliefs we hold. Hence why a left leaning person might only choose to watch MSNBC while a more conservative person may only choose to watch Fox News. In both cases the person is looking for stories that support their beliefs. It's uncomfortable to be presented with information that could potentially corrupt our supposedly objective beliefs. We then make an effort to avoid all sources of information that could jeopardize our sense of mental accuracy.

Ostrich Effect

We tend to bury our heads in the sand like an ostrich when presented with information that contradicts our beliefs or when presented with bad news. A person who refuses to check their mail out of fear there will be a bill or a parking ticket in their mailbox is victim to this cognitive bias. Simply put, it's a defense mechanism that the mind uses. Negative or disruptive information is a

threat to your mind's wellness, and the brain will sometimes engage the ostrich effect in an effort to protect its current positive
state. Far better for the mind not to notice the bad news at all
rather than be forced to process it, is the reasoning behind the
ostrich effect.

Outcome Bias

We have a tendency to judge the validity of a decision based on its
outcome rather than the decision itself. If we wage war against
another nation and win, the masses will tend to think that the
decision to go to war was smart one because the outcome was
victory. If we lose the war, the masses will tend to think that the
decision to wage war was a bad choice. Rather than examining
the decisions itself, we put more emphasis on the outcome.

Overconfidence

Many people are far more confident in their own abilities and
opinions than their actual abilities. There's nothing wrong with
confidence but unrealistic self-judgement will sometimes lead us
to form opinions that aren't accurate. Most of the time this is
harmless but at times our overconfidence can lead to highly inaccurate perceptions. For example, we might read a book on
trading and draw the conclusion that we are more knowledgeable about stock trading than we really are. This might cause us
to make risky financial decisions. Another part of this bias occurs
with industry "experts". When someone is labelled an expert in
any field, their own sense of self-importance is elevated to the extent that they will trust their own opinion over others whom may
be more knowledgeable. There are instances when the inability
to place value on outside sources of information could be cata-
strophic. Imagine a medical doctor who places very little value
on the opinion of the patient. The patient's opinion may not be
as highly valued because they don't have a degree in medicine.
However, the patient, knowing their own body, is in a position

to provide a much more accurate assessment of their condition. Ignoring or not lending adequate credence to the opinion of the patient may result in a misdiagnosis.

Placebo Effect

Of all the cognitive biases that psychologists have identified, the placebo effect is the one most useful to us because we can use it to hack our own beliefs for positive benefit. The placebo effect is the one bias that really taps into the power of the Law of Attraction. Medical doctors have long observed that patients will oftentimes recover from a disease when given a placebo such as a sugar pill. In many studies the placebo has been found to be more effective than the active substance in preventing and curing the disease. The placebo effect is an incredible scientific and objective example of the power of our beliefs. Our beliefs are directly tied to our physical and mental states. A 2004 study which appeared in the British Medical Journal, looked at the prescribing patterns of Danish physicians and found that 48% had prescribed a placebo at least ten times within the last year. When the researchers questioned a group of these doctors as to why they felt the need to prescribe placebos to their patients, the overall response was simply *"because they work, we can't explain why they work, but they do work to cure the patient."*

The reason that placebos can be so effective is due to the mechanics of the Law of Attraction. When a physician gives a patient a placebo, the patient generates a strong belief that they are taking something which will cure their condition. This strong belief generates thought energy to the universe to which the universe responds by manifesting wellness in your body.

The placebo effect doesn't work for everyone. Only about 30% of the world's population responds to placebos. In this 30% of people, their minds are open and receptive to the idea that they can be healed. If you are locked into a purely empirical and rigid way of thinking, you will miss out on the incredible effects that the Law of Attraction can bring into your life. In other words, if you have to see it to believe it, you won't reap the rewards. With the Law of Attraction, we must align our minds to believe in things we oftentimes cannot see or feel. This requires a certain degree of faith. The power of faith has been proven in clinical trials to cure or improve viral diseases, depression, and even Parkinson's disease.

Pro-innovation bias

Have you ever wondered why you oftentimes see the word "NEW!" on products in the grocery store? Manufactures have figured out that they can exploit our pro-innovation bias by labelling something as new or innovative. We have a tendency to automatically think that because something is new or has a slightly adjusted formulation that it will be better. This bias is grounded in the idea that technology always advances us toward something more useful. Oftentimes, innovation leads us in a direction that doesn't necessarily improve our lives. That doesn't stop us from becoming really excited about new things though. This bias lends us to believe that 100% of new ideas and products are good for us.

In 1961, a German company began mass production of an amphibious car that promised to allow a driver unlimited access across roads or waterways. At the time, the innovation seemed to herald the dawning of a new age of transportation and offered limitless freedom to travelers. Marketed primarily to drivers in the USA, the car was widely viewed as state of the art technology that would fundamentally change personal transportation. In reality, the functionality of a car/boat hybrid proved to be far less useful than the hype suggested, and the amphicar became a historical novelty rather than a truly useful way to get around. History is full of technological marvels that have promised to improve our lives which turned out to be huge flops. This won't stop us from wanting the latest and greatest smart phone or watch. Just knowing that something is new and innovative draws us to it with the assumption that it will be useful.

Recency

This bias involves our tendency to weigh more favorably the newest information we receive over older data. It is related to the pro-innovation bias in that we assume that newer is better. We tend to do this when analyzing trends and especially when looking at quantitative data. For example, it's very common for investors to look at current stock prices and trends and wrongly perceive that a stock will rise or fall. A more accurate analysis would be to examine the long term behavior of the stock and make a decision from the historical data. For example, when gold prices rise, it oftentimes results in a bubble from investors rushing to buy up gold. The price of gold is artificially inflated, and at some point the bubble bursts. We also saw this bias in effect recently when the value of a bitcoin rose to ridiculous numbers. When the digital currency was released in 2010, the value of 1 bitcoin equaled approximately 5 cents USD. Three years later, the value had skyrocketed to more than $1200 USD for 1 bitcoin. That's a 5000% increase in value over 3 years. These sorts of bubbles always pop and go through an adjustment phase. They are usually caused when public investors see what's currently happening within the market, and assume that increasing value is part of a new paradigm. In reality, they are being deluded by their recency bias and make the poor decision to buy at the artificially inflated price.

Selective perception

This is the tendency for one to view the world according to the expectations they hold. In a way, this a restating of the Law of Attraction. You've probably heard the term "self-fulfilling prophecy"? If you think that the world is out to get you, it will be. Our reality is the culmination of our perceptions. In the coming chapters we will examine more deeply how our beliefs act as perceptual filters which alter the judgements we make about the world.

Stereotyping

This bias has received a bad rap over the years. Stereotyping is part of our evolutionary defense mechanisms to help us identify friend or foe. Throughout our biologically evolved history, we have had to quickly make quick decisions about a potential friend or foe. Stereotyping allows us to look at an individual and ascribe a certain set of beliefs, ideas, tactics, and opinions. The reality of stereotypes is that sometimes they are correct! For instance, if you see a man walking down the street in a priest outfit, there's a good chance he is a person of faith. There's also a good chance he is caring, thoughtful, and kind to others. But, he might not be. He could be a bank robber in a disguise. He could be a disgruntled priest who uses his position to prey on the vulnerable. The danger comes when we rely too heavily on stereotypical thinking and assign negative traits to people when it's not deserved. The reverse is true as well - we may assign positive traits to an individual based on their appearance that are undeserved. An obvious example is white privilege.

Ok so my Thinking is Highly Biased, What Now?

With all these innate biases in effect, you might wonder how our brains could possibly develop an accurate view of the world at all. How is it that our minds construct a seemingly objective reality in which we function and thrive? Can we trust our brains to present us with accurate and objective data about our environment? The short answer is no. The perceptions, beliefs, and inferences we make about the world and about others are highly subjective and therefore are prone to disillusion. We have ultimate control over the way we choose to process reality. One person's trash is another person's treasure. What one person sees as a hopeless situation, another person may see as a wonderful opportunity. We can **choose** to view the world in terms which will be positive for us, or we can **choose** to view the world in terms that will hurt us and inhibit the manifestation of good things in our lives. Since you have ultimate control over the filters, beliefs, and innate biases of your own mind, you are the only one making the choice. **Your state of mind is completely up to you.**

The incredible news is that once we understand how our beliefs function as filters that our brain uses to process limited information, we can begin to hack this system to our immediate and dramatic benefit. In the next chapter, I will tell you step by step how to accomplish this.

Whatever you can dream and whatever your goals, it can easily and quickly be achieved through hacking our own mind bias. Belief transformation, unwavering faith, and directed action will all serve vital roles in this process. Open your mind and prepare to have your world radically changed for the better as we examine the powerful and simple techniques ahead. Welcome to a new world where anything you desire is possible!

EXERCISE 2

Take out a separate sheet of paper and make three columns. At the top of column one, write "Life Area". In the middle column, write "Limiting Belief". At the top of the last column, write "Unlimited Belief".

In the left hand column, write out the following life areas, using one row for each:

- Physical Health

- Spiritual Health

- Financial Health

- Friends and Family

- Significant Other

- Career/ Professional Development

- My Contribution to the World

In the middle column, under "Limiting Beliefs", write down any limiting beliefs you currently hold in regards to each of these life areas. Feel free to add additional life areas that may be of importance to you.

Put an X through each limiting belief that you just wrote down. Don't worry, you won't be needing these again.

In the last column, choose a new belief to replace your limiting belief in each of these areas. Then go back and read each new, empowering belief with as much feeling and commitment as possible. Allow yourself to feel the excitement that taking on this new belief brings. Think about how your life has instantly changed as a result of this new belief. Imagine what actions you will now take with your new belief.

Refer back to this paper often to reaffirm your new beliefs and to feel the emotions associated with it.

Chapter 7: How and Why to Meditate

There's been thousands of clinical studies conducted on meditation and its effects on the human brain. Practitioners report a wide range of experiences. A common occurrence resulting from practicing meditation daily is that people start to care about others more and spontaneously feel compassion, especially to those whom they used to find egocentric or offensive in some way. Why do these feelings of empathy emerge when we practice meditation daily?

When we connect with the true self consistently, we start to understand that we are all spiritual beings, independent of social status or external objects like houses and cars. Out true identity as a human being is a spiritual identity. The big you, or sometimes called the ego, is only concerned with external sources of support and validation. The true self comes from pure energy and love; it is actually the universe within you, or you could even call it God. Understanding this allows you to identify and see right through an egocentric person's veil of supremacy for what it is — a desperate attempt to prop up their ego through sources of external validation. This realization allows us to see people for who they truly are - not for their looks, their car, or how big their house is. After a few months meditating, you will be able to look into the eyes of other people, and feel their inner presence - their pure, small, divine energy that is total love and joy. Understanding that egos are simply the big you in action, allows you to forgive egocentric and selfish behavior in a way that was not possible before developing a mindful meditation practice.

How Exactly Do I Meditate to Achieve Results?

I would be remiss if I didn't include a solid instruction on meditation. With all this talk of the benefits, it's important that you know how to go about it for maximum and speedy results. If you are an experienced meditator, feel free to skip ahead to the next chapter. Even if you are experienced with meditation, feel free to keep reading to get my take on the practice as it relates to the Law of Attraction. In order to effectively manifest things, people, or places into our lives, we must first be aligned with the universe. This process of alignment naturally occurs through a daily meditative practice. After a few months of meditation, you will begin to have new insights and a peaceful understanding of reality unlike anything you've ever experienced.

Exercise for the Mind

We learn in meditation to control the mind. We learn that time is subjective, and that the most important point in time is the current moment. Our existence is simply a series of present moments; each one a treasure to appreciate. Because we have been conditioned from childhood to live within the control of the ego or false self, we must unlearn the mind chatter and yearning of the ego. It's difficult at first so we start slow and for practice for short intervals. As you gain greater and greater levels of control over your mind, you will find that your meditation sessions become easier and much more enjoyable.

How to Meditate

- Find a quiet area in your home. Make sure all distractions are out of the room - pets and other family members. Close the windows and doors to keep excessive noise out.

- Sit on the floor, legs crossed and arms gently resting on your knees. I like to sit on a pillow since I find this more comfortable. You may also wish to place small pillows under your ankles for additional comfort. I like to sit with legs crossed and the back straight and unsupported. If you have back issues, you may want to use a wall or even purchase a special chair designed just for meditation.

- Set an alarm. I use my cell phone and sit in close enough that I will hear the alarm go off when the time is up. If you are a beginner, start with a 5 minute meditation. As you progress, you can gradually lengthen your sessions up to 45 minutess or more. I normally meditate twice a day for 20-30 minute sessions. I find the longer I meditate, the more intense and lasting the benefits.

- Close your eyes. Focus only on your breath. Breathe in your nose and out your mouth.

- Attempt to empty your mind of chatter. At first, this will seem impossible. It may take a while to be able to do this - be patient and stick with it. I guarantee the results are worth it! After several weeks of practice you will notice that your mind begins to naturally settle during your sessions. Do not attempt to block out wild thoughts - only focus on the present moment. This means that the goal is not to think about your day at work, or that research project that is overdue. When thoughts do arise, simply observe them non-judgmentally and allow them to pass. Gently and easily accept all that comes into your mind, however, make a conscious effort to feel and experience the present moment. This means that you are highly aware of your own breathing and physical sensations within your body. Feel the weight of your body on the pillow. Fully experience the now and allow yourself to relax. Strive for an empty mind. Observe all thoughts non-judgmentally. Just breathe.

- When the alarm goes off, open your eyes. It's that simple.

Keep at It

Every meditation session will be different. Sometimes you may not be able to stop the chatter and other times you may slip effortlessly into a state of now that is blissful and refreshing. Meditation can be compared to golf; some days you might have a great game and shoot near or under par while other days you may donate a few balls to the water hazards and sand traps. As long you keep playing, you will get better. Golfers who play will become more consistent in their game. So too with meditation - the more you meditate, the more consistent your experience becomes. Give yourself several months of daily meditation before expecting to see consistency. You will however, begin to feel the benefits within a few short weeks.

When you first start meditating, the ego may freak out and attempt to bombard your mind with worry, projections of the future, or present you with emotionally difficult memories from your past. This is a good thing – it's part of the process and means that you are starting to shift closer to experiencing the real you. The ego is being broken down, meditation by meditation - it is losing control of you and will fight to gain its power back. Simply recognize this for what it is - observe it as an external part of your mind and allow any memories, emotions, or chatter to pass. Allow yourself to fully feel any emotions that arise; do not attempt to suppress them. It may help to use the Green Blob Method to process emotions that I described earlier.

I find it best to sit in silence, focus on the present moment, and just clear my mind.

The Emergence of Your True Self

Eventually, something miraculous will happen. You will feel your true self come through. This will feel like a deep, cool, refreshing source of infinite universal energy that transcends every concept you have of your physical self. It's as if you are experiencing your pure eternal nature; a pureness that lives outside the confines of physical form. The true self emerges when our minds are not preoccupied and busy with propping up and supporting the ego. The big you/ego only lives in the world of our thoughts.

With more and more practice, you'll find that it becomes easier to move into the experience of the true self. You will leave your meditations with a renewed love for life, gratitude beyond words, and a deep well of peace that overflows continually. I know, that sounds like some hefty promises but I assure you that you will experience this too if you approach your meditation practice with some patience and an open heart.

EXERCISE 3

Follow the above procedure to practice a mindful meditation session. Notice any distractions or wandering of the mind throughout the process. Accept any feelings of nervousness or excessive thinking. The first few weeks of meditation are the hardest, so during this time accept all that comes into your mind as normal and part of the process. Start with a simple five minute meditation. After the meditation, take some time to write down how you feel. Choose five emotions and write them down. Each time you meditate, write down how you feel after. Writing down five emotions immediately after meditation helps you to connect with how you are feeling and serves as a written reminder of how you are progressing in your practice.

CHAPTER 8: THE MECHANICS OF THE LAW OF ATTRACTION - HOW IT WORKS

"If you can dream it, you can do it." - Walt Disney

"The thing always happens that you really believe in; and the belief in a thing makes it happen." - Frank Lloyd Wright

The Law of Attraction simply states that like attracts like. When you think a thought, it generates vibrational energy that is sent out into the universe. In response, the universe returns information that coincides with that thought. If we think positive things, we will see positive things manifest in our lives. Adversely, if we think negative thoughts, we will attract more negative people and circumstances into our lives.

Thus, it is important that we continually and purposefully seek out positive feelings and situations. It is our responsibility to fill our lives with joy through laughter, fun, and stress reduction. In the coming chapters, you will complete an exercise which helps you to identify those negative situations or people in your life that may be causing you harm. It is critical that negativity is eliminated from your daily life.

Focus only on the things which bring you happiness and joy. Right at this moment, you likely have many things in your life that are contributing to negative energy. Even non-conscious objects have their own energy. Start with a thorough house-cleansing. Go through each room of your house and touch and examine every physical thing you own. If the object does not bring you a sense of joy or appreciation, throw it away. Do not cling to physical objects which serve no purpose. If you haven't used something in six months, toss it out. (Excluding seasonal clothing and gear of course).

Identifying Negative People in Our Lives

If we are mediating daily and connecting with our true self, we should become nearly impervious to attacks directed at our ego, since we are no longer using the false self to define who we really are. When ego isn't guiding us, we can see the good in bad people. Sometimes though, a person in your life may be so narcissistic or scheming that they can cause you serious social or even physical harm. Even though you may be emotionally resilient and somewhat impervious to their attacks, narcissistic people have the desire to chronically and systematically destroy you through various deceptive means. This type of person is devoid of empathy and only thinks of their own gain.

Having a friend who is an occasional Debbie Downer is no reason to reject him or her from your life. To the contrary, your positive spirit and mindful state can help you bring them out of their funk and move them towards a better state of mind. When I refer to *negative people*, I'm referring to the people you've identified who have the potential to harm your career, family, livelihood, or health. These people are living so far within their egos they can only view you as an object to validate their sense of false superiority. Narcissists will stop at nothing to prove this false superiority, and they are ultimately dangerous people. It is up to you to decide whether a person in your life fits into this category. The exercise at the end of this chapter should help you to do so.

This type of negative person in your life must be pruned from your social circle. For negative family members or bosses, you can use the Law of Attraction to mitigate the potential harm and to highlight the good within them. Do not try to change people; you cannot control others using the Law of Attraction. It is far better to cut ties quickly with someone deemed a chronic negative energy producer rather than attempt to persuade or mold that person into something they're not. Each conscious entity has control over their own mind, and must take their own responsibility to operate within a positive frame. There are some chronically negative people who will use manipulation, lies, and social leveraging to solidify their own sense of importance. Their egos are so strong that they will go to any means to protect it. This means that they will not hesitate to use and abuse you for their own ego-boosting and maintenance purposes. Identifying these energy suckers is vitally important to your success.

The Dangers of Social Media in a Big You World

Social media has the potential to generate feelings of bonding, love, connection, and friendship. More likely though, social media tends to create feelings of jealousy, envy, greed, and even hatred. Today's typical Facebook user scrolls through their news feed as a means to compare others with themselves. Commonly, social media is a source of information gathering and gossip for our "frenemies". Recent studies have shown that Facebook users visit most often the pages of those people whom they hold in either high or low regard. Users will check out the pages of those friends whom they secretly hate *or* those whom they really love. The folks in the middle of the affection spectrum are followed the least. What this means is that we tend to see strong polarising forces develop within social media. From some people you will receive overwhelming support and encouragement while from others you will see trolling, blatantly negative or solicitous comments, and/or a general sense of maliciousness. More obvious energy suckers will exhibit blatantly offensive behaviour, such as never liking your status updates, yet always liking any comment that casts you in a negative light. These people have learned to derive their sense of worth from putting others down. They serve no purpose in your life. Limit their ability to do you harm and refuse to become their ego boost. Once exposed, these negative entities are easily contained just by ignoring them and placing no value on their actions or words. In some cases, you may find it socially beneficial to keep these people around as friends on social media. In this case, make sure to unsubscribe from their updates and restrict their access to your information. Usually, these individuals are not very present and will have no idea that you've essentially eliminated their negative influence from your life.

Don't Dwell on Negative Subjects

Avoid negative news stories and documentaries. It may be a good idea to avoid the news altogether since it is almost entirely negative. It is perfectly fine to stay informed with world events but do not dwell on them. Tragedies come and go. They are not something that will be beneficial to generating constant positive energy.

Understanding the Law of Attraction is essential to creating our own reality. We can have, do, or be anything that we desire. Of most significance is the ability to understand how limiting beliefs, which I call negative *mind bias*, serves to undermine the manifestation of your goals. By hacking our mind bias, we can come to expect only the good things in our lives, and the universe will deliver every time.

Hard Science Doesn't Offer a Complete Understanding

If you have even a small amount of scientific training, you will understand the differences between a hypothesis, a theory, and a law. For something to be called a *law* in science, it means that it has passed an extremely high level of empirical scrutiny. It means that it has been tested over and over and over again and found to always hold true.

Science is a wonderful thing and helps us to build skyscrapers, search the ocean floor, and put a man on the moon. One big problem that science has is that it only deals with information collected from our senses. Ultimately, all scientific endeavors rely on a human to examine the information and draw conclusions based on observable experimentation. This means that science as we know it is extremely limited in its ability to understand reality. What if there are forces and dimensions all around us that we cannot see because we do not have the necessary sense organs to do so? We can't make the assumption this isn't possible. In fact, it is much more likely there are extra dimensions beyond those in which we operate and unseen forces shape our reality in ways we can only imagine. Developing a scientific world views means that we look at the world solely through the empirical data presented to our senses. This is a limited data set and cannot offer complete explanations for the human experience.

The Law of Attraction is Not Science as We Know It

We call the Law of Attraction a *law* because it has been found to consistently hold true both through personal stories and experimentation. We describe the energy which thoughts generate as a vibrational force because this concept is easily understood. We have no discernible way of measuring these vibrational waves, but we assume that something along these lines is being generated. Attempting to use the scientific method to explain the Law of Attraction is pointless and will only lead to confusion. It is best to examine the Law of Attraction in terms of notional concepts rather than applying what we know of as hard science. Some may argue that this discredits or limits the credibility of the Law of Attraction however, this is only because they have a mind bias that says "*only empirical science as we know it is a valid method to explain reality*". This is a very limiting position, in that it does not account for the myriad of conditions that cannot be explained through traditional scientific reasoning. For the doubters, I will present the problem of consciousness itself, which many argue cannot be described within the confines of traditional scientific query. To understand consciousness, we must entertain the idea of a new way of thinking which accounts for the possibility of unobservable data beyond the capabilities of our sense perceptions.

Science Can't Provide all the Answers

Scientists don't hold a monopoly on coming up with hypotheses. Even with a layman's understanding of quantum theory, we can draw inferences and see some potential meaning in the bigger picture. It's not a scientific approach by the standards of the scientific method, however, we're thinking about things that admittedly, may not be logical and may not fit within the normal confines of rational procedure. This being the case, I think it's perfectly fine that we take a very unscientific look at what the modern study of the quantum world has found and we can then draw our own conclusions as to the significance of those findings.

How small is the quantum world? It's much, much smaller than what we think of we talk about sub-atomic particles. The quantum world is really just information stored as energy. Mother Nature never intended primates to peek into this space behind the curtain of physical space. Our sensory inputs and brain work together to construct a sense of reality that is based on traditional or what is called *macro physics*. Through technology, we've been able to do what our evolution never designed us to do – take a peek at this very strange and very small quantum reality.

The most interesting thing scientists find when they observe the quantum world is that our brains are intrinsically linked to it. Physical matter actually requires a human consciousness to exist as something with mass. Without a conscious entity observing the object, it collapses into an energy potential.

This was proven way back in the 1920s by Einstein in the famous double-slit experiment. I won't cover the details of that experiment in this book as it's beyond the scope of our discussion however if you aren't familiar with it I highly encourage you to google it. There are some great YouTube videos which use animation to explain this famous experiment. For now, you should understand that essentially what the experiment showed Einstein was that particles exist only as an energy potential until they are directly observed by a conscious mind.

How incredible is that? What is the significance of that fact alone? The Law of Attraction teaches that "thoughts become things". It also teaches us that our thoughts exist as vibrational energy, and that this energy interacts with our external reality. Since we know from the double-slit experiment that consciousness and reality are interdependent of one-another, this lends enormous credibility to the Law of Attraction as a physical phenomenon. **The real significance of the double-slit experiment is that we can infer that our minds are directly responsible in some way for our external reality and that we have the ability, through controlling our thoughts and feelings, to manipulate our personal reality.**

I won't pretend to be a mathematician. I can't dive into the nitty gritty details of quantum mathematics. But what I can tell you, is that everything that we see coming from the scientific study of the quantum world, including the more recent string and M theories, strongly supports the concepts which make up the Law of Attraction.

Love is a Quantum Entanglement of Mind and Body

I was recently talking with a work colleague and he mentioned that he felt that he and wife were somehow connected and that he could sense when she had a problem even though he was currently in Germany and she was in Texas. He said that he felt that they were quantumly entangled somehow. At first I thought this was humorous if not romantic but a few months after having this conversation, I came across an article in Scientific American in which researchers had observed for the first time quantum effects on macro objects. Love is a mysterious thing, and we've all had instances where we felt an otherworldly connection to a significant other. Researchers from the University of Oxford, the National Research Council of Canada and the National University of Singapore (NUS) were able to link two naked-eye diamonds through quantum entanglement at room temperature. This experiment marked the first time that scientists were able to entangle particles between two normal objects that you can hold in your hand. Prior to this experiment, quantum entanglement had only been achieved with super small subatomic particles and only then in extremely cold conditions. The significance of this achievement tells us something profound about our natural world – the quantum weirdness that we observe in sub atomic objects can be extended to the normal world, to include human bodies and minds. There is not really a separate set of rules and physics for very small things and normal world things – we are all bound by the same law.

Human beings can become entangled. When two objects are entangled, whatever happens to one effects the other. Distance is not a concern. We could be light years apart and yet our particles will be linked. Whenever one particle is changed, it instantly affects the other. This is why love lingers, why there's an intrinsic connection to your family members, and ultimately why you can build such a deep connection with other people regardless of distances involved. Once again, science is lending credibility to the law of Attraction. Our form of science can't currently explain everything, but that shouldn't stop us from learning how to hack the system *now* for our immediate benefit.

Embodied Cognition

It is becoming clear to scientists who attempt to study the mysterious realm of human consciousness and cognition that the mind is shaped by much more than the brain and our central nervous system. A new area of research is gaining traction and legitimacy in the scientific community known as embodied cognition. Psychologists, sociologists, and medical researchers have observed from time to time over decades of research that there are sometimes undeniable, objective, and empirical evidence of cognition extension beyond the confines of the human brain.

One shocking and clear example of EC is something called "enclothed cognition". Scientific experiments have proven beyond a shadow of a doubt that what we actually choose to wear can have direct and powerful effects on our cognition. These effects extend to our emotional states, our ability to memorize facts, and our ability to process information. EC is stark and solid evidence of the law of attraction in action. Proving that human consciousness is tied to external factors such as clothing, place, lighting, color, and the minds of other people shatters our traditionally held beliefs about the mind. (You may sometimes hear this referred to in mindfulness literature "non-local consciousness").

In a recent 2012 study, researchers at Northwestern University proved in a series of experiments that the clothes we choose to wear can directly impact our mental processes. They describe this phenomenon as *enclothed cognition*. In their first experiment, subjects were given a white lab coat to wear and then given a series of tasks to complete which required memory and attention to detail. The researchers found that those people who wore the lab coats did significantly better than a control group who did not wear white lab coats.

In their second experiment, the researchers gave everyone white lab coats to wear while completing the tasks. This time, the control group was told that the white coat was a painter's jacket, and the other group was told that the white coat was a doctor's lab coat. You can probably guess the results. The group who believed they were wearing the doctor's coat scored significantly higher than the control group once again.

The researchers repeated the experiments over and over, with completely different groups, and always got the same outcome. What was most puzzling to the researchers was how simply wearing an item of clothing seemed to improve cognitive functioning. Beyond a shadow of a doubt, those who wore the doctor's white lab coat had temporarily improved their intelligence. This incredible discovery led to an earnest search for a reasonable explanation. The only conclusions the researchers were able to draw was that the ability of certain types of clothing to increase cognitive ability relied heavily on two factors: 1) the symbolic meaning of the clothing to the wearer, and 2) the physical experience of wearing the clothes.

What does this phenomenon of enclothed cognition tell us about our minds and the way our consciousness interacts with the world? It's easy to see from these experiments that our thoughts have a direct and profound influence on our cognitive condition. This means that what we think, we become. The researchers at Northwestern University could never come out and say this, because it defies the boundaries of the scientific method. This is but one example of many where the scientific method fails to offer an explanation to situations that cannot be explained without acknowledging unknown or unseen forces at work. Those unknown forces here are the Law of Attraction in action.

When we look at the enclothed cognition phenomenon from a Law of Attraction perspective, we can explain it rather easily. Consciousness is non-local, meaning that your consciousness is influenced and shaped by the things and people around you. Everything in this universe has vibrational energy. Conscious beings are a complex collection of strong and weak vibrational forces interacting with the vibrations and feelings of the objects and people around them. When subjects donned what they believed to be a doctor's coat, they were drawing on the symbolic associations of the clothing to shape their own cognition. The key element here is belief. Each subject in the experiment held a strong belief which they associated with the lab coat. That belief temporarily formed their reality. Because the subjects were creating vibrational energy that said, *"I am intelligent, I am scholarly, I am a doctor"*; the universe responded in kind and manifested reality to match their beliefs.

Evidence of the Law of Attraction in Modern Physics

"Look deep into nature, and then you will understand everything better". – Albert Einstein

When we look at the history of science, we see man's attempt to explain the natural world. The original science was religion. Religion began as a set of ideas, stories, and rules that man used to describe and make sense of the natural world. As mankind developed rational and more accurate tools which acknowledged the limitations of our own biased reasoning, we began to accelerate our understanding of the natural world through rational study. Thus, we moved away from religion as we know it toward a new religion; the religion known as science.

Science is simply a religion which uses the scientific method in an attempt to draw conclusions which are less unadulterated by innate human biases. Many scientists cling to this with an iron grip, dismissing anything that falls outside the confines of the type of reasoning that fits within the limitations of the scientific method. How can the scientific method be limiting or confine us to certain ways of thought? There are many examples including Bell's theorem, quantum entanglement, the observer effect, and many others. Quantum entanglement, an action on one object directly affecting another object immediately even if that object is a billion miles away, cannot be explained without admitting that something exists beyond our understanding. The scientific method cannot provide an answer because the scientific method relies on empirical observation at the macro level and assumes that the world behaves according to the rules of classical physics. Bell's theorem was perhaps the most significant discovery of the twentieth century because it shows that quantum entanglement cannot happen without the existence of non-local or non-observable forces.

The modern study of quantum mechanics offers some interesting parallels between the concept of our thoughts as vibrational energy and current theories regarding the quantum world. Before we jump too deep into this subject, I should note that I'm not making any outlandish claims as some books do. I'm simply saying that we can observe some interesting similarities here that lend credibility to the idea of thoughts as energy.

The Traditional Model

You may have been exposed to the Law of Attraction in the past, and the three step process by which you can use to manifest your desires. This is a valid process and highly effective, but I believe that it does not tell the whole story. The Law of Attraction tells us that manifestation occurs when we do the following:

- Ask

- Believe

- Receive

This process is entirely correct, but it's really a simple overview of the way things work. To really be effective, we need examine step

2 and drill down a bit deeper, as well as understand the importance of directed action. It is my belief that many people attempt to use the Law of Attraction and fail simply because they do not fully comprehend the importance of step 2. In order to manifest effectively every time, you must believe with every core of your being that your desire will come true in the near future. Additionally, you must be willing to act. Action comes in the form of inspiration and directed purpose. We will examine each of these in the coming chapters. Once we have manifested our desires, we also must continue to generate positive thought energy and prevent the tendency to revert back to long held negative mind biases. Maintenance and adjustment of our reality is an important additional step.

Beliefs are like Tracks on a Record

Beliefs are not easily changed. Our brains want to cling to beliefs for years because beliefs serve as the template by which the mind makes sense of the world when it has limited data to work with. Beliefs that you've held since childhood are ingrained in your thinking and have become habitual. You likely have beliefs right now that are limiting your progress toward manifesting your dreams.

Many may approach the law of attraction with an optimistic heart, but upon greater examination of their core beliefs, we find that they hold an underlying belief of skepticism. This underlying core belief is working against the Law of Attraction and preventing manifestation of positive things. The first step in solving any problem is identifying the problem. Identifying your core beliefs about each desire is critical to manifestation. If we encounter a limiting belief, we must hack our mind bias so that manifestation is more likely to occur.

In addition to hacking our mind bias, we must also take directed and inspired action. Once we have corrected our beliefs to coincide with our goals, we must then act upon those beliefs. For example, if I believe with all my heart that I will have ten million dollars in the bank by the end of the year, I must then be ready and willing to take inspired action toward that goal when the universe presents an opportunity. Once the unwavering faith is there, the universe will always show you the way.

The Complete Model

1. **Ask**

2. **Unwavering Faith**

3. identify limiting beliefs

4. belief transformation

5. generate the feelings of having it now

6. **Act**

7. directed action

8. inspired action

9. **Receive**

10. **Maintain and Adjust**

Now that you know the process in a more detailed form, let's examine each step on the path to manifestation.

CHAPTER 9: DECIDE WHAT YOU WANT

"As far as I can tell, it's just about letting the universe know what you want, working toward it while letting go of how it comes to pass" – Jim Carrey

"People who ask confidently get more than those who are hesitant and uncertain. When you've figured out what you want to ask for, do it with certainty, boldness and confidence."– Jack Canfield

This is the fun part! Sit down with a hot cup of tea or your favorite adult beverage of choice and a notebook and begin to write down everything you desire in your life. No dream is too big. No one needs to see this list; keep it private if possible. Think about each area of your life - friends, family, career, love - write down your biggest desire for each area.

Most people have no problems with the asking part. Feel free to ask for everything, and to never think a wish is too small or too big.

You really need to fathom the significance of this step. Whatever you ask for at this point will at some point in the future manifest into your life. You should understand that you must be absolutely sure this is what you want. The universe will deliver your request as long as the other parts of the formula are met. This means that when we ask, we need to be very specific. We also need to take time to fully appreciate how things will change once the goal is manifested. For example, if you ask for a new car, don't just ask for a new car with leather interior and a moon roof. You need to ask for the specific model, color, interior color, options, and price. Being very specific when we ask helps to ensure that we are satisfied with our manifestations and that we are capable of living with them.

Know Where you are Coming From

An unstated precursor to asking the universe is acceptance of your current state. No one ever really talks about this but it's important to understand. When you are asking, it is because you feel in your heart that you are lacking something whether that be a person, situation, or level of economic gain. First fully accept the truth of your current situation. You might be broke, homeless, or have no friends. Pretending this isn't your current reality is just stupid. Accept the brutal truth of your situation. Only by accepting the truth can you *change* the truth. A drug addict cannot change until they first acknowledge that they are an addict. As you begin to fully accept where you are, you can then get excited about the rapid change that will soon happen. Part of the process will be to generate feelings as if you already have what you want. This isn't about fooling yourself - you always want to dwell in truth. The positive feelings of having it now will cause your reality to radically change. Always dwell in truth.

Ask by Giving Thanks

Keep in mind that the word "ask" is a bit misleading in this step. You're not asking in the typical sense. Rather, you are making a statement to the universe concerning your desire. This statement does not come in the form of "*I want a new car.*" Additionally, you are not asking in the future tense. The way we ask using the Law of Attraction is to make a proclamation of gratitude to the universe concerning the object, situation, or person of your desire. For example, you would ask for a new car in the following way: "*I am so happy and grateful now that I drive a brand new Porsche Panamera*". Notice that the statement is very specific and is in the present tense. You already possess the object of your desire, it just has not yet manifested in your life. It is, however, on its way.

The reason that we don't ask in the normal sense is that when you say something to the universe to the effect of, "*I wish I had a new car*", or "*I want a new car*", what you are focusing on is the fact that you currently do not have a new car. By focusing on lack, we receive lack in return. The universe exactly mirrors the thought energy we generate. As such, it's very important that we ask in an exact and mindful way. Our requests must be in the form of present statements of gratitude.

Embrace Abundance When Asking

Before we jump to the exciting part where you begin to use the Law of Attraction as your own universal shopping spree, take a moment to think about the things that you really want in life. If our end goal is to be happy, loved, valued, and to enjoy all that life can offer then we may unknowingly end up asking for things which we already possess. You heard me right - many times we seek external sources to bring us what we want and ignore what's right in front of us. Do you have a loving family and supportive friends? Do you live in a beautiful city? Can you generate enough income to feed and clothe yourself? On the surface, it may seem that following such a line of questioning is focusing on the low-hanging fruit, since we are not seeking flashy new cars and riches, but after some time alone connecting with our true self, we usually find that our motivations begin to change. We often find that the motivation behind wanting to be rich comes from a real desire to be loved and accepted.

When we connect with our true spiritual self through mindful meditative practice, we discover something unique, incredible, and greater than any possession you could possibly obtain on Earth. We discover the still small spirit inside ourselves that actually *is* the universe. You discover that the big you is not really that important in the grand scheme. Material possessions can be nice in the sense that they provide meaningful function, and sometimes can provide gratuitous fun, but they will never provide the sense of love that a loyal life companion brings when he or she stares into your eyes and tells you they love you. A new car will not bring the sense of joy that watching your children grow into adulthood brings. Diamonds and gold will not replicate the simple act of cuddling up on the couch to watch a movie with your significant other. These experiences are intangibles - they cannot be bought. Seeking happiness through the acquisition of wealth or possessions is like chasing a carrot on a stick. True happiness, peace, and life contentment come when we realise that not only will the universe provide all that we need but that in many ways, it already has given what we really need.

EXERCISE 4

Now that I've given you the prerequisite warning, it's time to start making our dreams a reality. It's time to ask for want you want.

Don't obsess over crafting the exact phrasing of your request. You can use the following sentence as a template for all of your requests:

"I am so happy and grateful now that X has come into my life." (Obviously, X will be the object, person, or situation of your desire)

Take a piece of blank paper and list everything you want to manifest right now in your life. Dream as big as you can. No desire is too ridiculous or unobtainable. If you follow the steps in this book all these goals will come true. Be careful with this! Make sure you really want each desire to come into your life and that you are ready to receive it. Do not wish for a new dog if you don't have the time or space to care for a dog properly. The universe will deliver on your desires whether you are ready for it or not. When you write these wishes out, write them as though they have already manifested in your life. For example, you might write something to the effect of: *"I am so ecstatic and joyous now that I am deeply loved and cared for by my beautiful significant other."*

Once you have all your desires written out, store them in a safe place as we will be coming back to each one in a later exercise. For each desire, we will be doing some powerful visualization techniques that generate enormous amounts of positive thought energy to the universe. In these visualizations, you will have the power to specify the specific details of each desire. For example, you will be able to choose the hair and/or eye color of your new boyfriend or girlfriend. The universe responds directly to your thought energy, and the better the resolution, the more likely the universe will deliver to you exactly what you want.

In further exercises, we will identify your current limiting beliefs that are hindering your ability to generate positive thought energy. We will take these limiting beliefs and transform them so at a fundamental level, you are always generating thought energy that is congruent with the manifestation of your desires.

Starting From a Positive Position

To really effectively manifest things into your life, you need to approach the 3 step process with a heart and mind of positivity. Throughout the believing and receiving stages, work to maintain a state of absolute positivity. This is sometimes easier said than done. If you are starting out from a particularly low energy level, you may feel helpless and unable to pull yourself out of the rut you're currently in. First, understand that everything that has happened in your life up until this exact moment in time has occurred for the sole purpose of bringing to your awareness the Law of Attraction and its power to transform your life. View the hardship and struggles of your past as lessons and life events for which you are supremely grateful. Your past has brought you to this present moment, which is the moment when your life begins to radically change for the better.

There are six things you can do to immediately shift into a positive state of being. These are very simple and effective and you can come back to this at any time for a positivity boost.

- Realize that you already are happy. When you mediate or just sit still and relax completely, you realize that happiness is actually your default state. Negativity and pessimism are constructions of the mind that infect your natural state of happiness. Simply realizing that you're natural state is one of happiness instantly shifts your thinking and externalizes negative thoughts, treating them as the foreign invaders they are.

- Listen to the negative narrative in your head. When we are in a negative state of being, we tend to have an ongoing narrative with our thoughts that colors all of our perceptions. Attempt to identify this negative self-talk. Once you see it, it starts to immediately lose its power. The simple act of observing the negative narrative serves to lessen its importance. As you continue to mediate daily, your ability to see this narrative will become stronger, and the narrative will have less and less control and importance to your sense of self.

- Take a quick inventory of your data inputs. Sounds like advice one would give to an android? Well, what I mean by this is that when you are in a negative state, you should think about the sources of information that you are feeding into your mind. Are you reading a book full of negative energy? Perhaps you are watching a TV show that is very dark with lots of negative themes? Do a quick inventory of your information sources and just eliminate those. It's like being exposed to a poison gas. If you can walk out of a room filled with poison gas into a room full of clean air, you will instantly be able to breathe.

- Stop what you're doing and *do* something that you *know* makes you happy. This could be painting, woodworking, writing short stories, running, golf, etc. Engage in a hobby that uses your creative mind, and generates feelings of positivity.

- Take out your wish list and imagine that you have all this *now*. This simple act will radically change your mental state to one of joy and gratitude. Think about that new Lambo or the beautiful husband or wife in your arms. Relish in the idea and *feeling* of having these things now in this present moment. You can use this technique as a way to shift instantly to a positive mind state.

- WRITE down 5 things that cause you to feel positive and joyful. Don't type them. Let's go old school analog with this and actually use a pen or pencil and a piece of paper! The physical act of writing things down makes you happy and joyful in the present moment.

Generate the Feelings of Having it Now

Faith is important, and we will jump deep into the aspects of faith in the next chapter. Right now, I want to share with you something that will result in an immediate and powerful realization of your manifestation goals. Throughout this book, the material you learn and the exercises you complete are geared toward putting you in a mindset that will enable you to consistently use the Law of Attraction to manifest people, places or situations into your life. You should read and reread this book until that mindset becomes second nature. For an immediate supercharge to your manifestation goals, I would like to introduce you to a very powerful weapon in your arsenal: Your emotions.

Why are emotions so effective in manifesting our wishes? Because an emotion is the most potent form of positive or negative vibrational thought energy that your mind can produce. Nothing is more effective and quick at producing results. Later on, we'll discuss visualization techniques that will help you to tap into the power of your emotions. For now, let's focus on one thing in your life that you want. Visualize and *feel* what it would be like to have your object of desire. Hold onto and cherish that feeling. Place yourself into a state of accepting that you currently hold this object of desire. Don't wish for it — just gently accept and strongly experience the emotions associated with having it now.

The deeper and more intense the feelings you create, the quicker you will see your desire manifest. Simply thinking about your desires won't do much because the level of vibrational energy is relatively low. When you actually *feel* your desires, you jumpstart the process. Emotions of *having it now* are the condensed and potent extension of normal thought energy.

———

Recently I caught myself ruminating about a perceived lack of friends who shared my interest in climbing. I would often want to go do some climbing on the cliffs in a nearby town. My thinking was going somewhere along the lines of *"It's so hard to get people to do anything requiring physical exertion."*, and *"People are so lazy"*. Along with these negative thoughts, I was experiencing feelings of loneliness, resentment, and frustration. I wanted my friends to be interested in climbing, and I was frustrated and up-set that I could not motivate anyone to climb with me. It didn't take long for me to come to the conclusion that my own thought energy was responsible for my current state. I sat down to medi-tate for 20 minutes and clear my mind of the negative thoughts. I began to allow myself to experience the feelings of having sev-eral friends text me, asking me to come climbing with them. I visualized my phone blowing up with invites, and visualized a weekly group of climbers meeting together at the local indoor gym. I saw and felt us laughing and climbing together. In those visualizations, some of the emotions I felt were joy, gratitude, self-worth, and a sense of belonging. I let those emotions settle in on me, and let them linger for a while. I left the meditation with a sense of satisfaction and ease.

Can you guess what started happening within the next few weeks? One friend from my ski club contacted me about climb-ing indoors at a local gym. She told me that she and her girlfriend attend every Monday there because it was ladies night and they climbed for half price. A buddy whom I had not talked to in a while contacted me a week later and invited me to climb with him. My girlfriend actually brought up climbing over dinner one night. Additionally, I discovered that there were great people in my social network who loved to climb, and that by putting forth a little effort (directed action), they were happy to meet up with me during the week and climb after work. Now, I have exactly what I allowed myself to feel - a group of friends I can hang with and climb with on a regular basis.

CHAPTER 10: UNWAVERING FAITH

"Faith is to believe what you do not see; the reward of this faith is to see what you believe". - Saint Augustine

"All who call on God in true faith, earnestly from the heart, will certainly be heard, and will receive what they have asked and desired."
- Martin Luther King

Faith is by far the most important ingredient in the Law of Attraction. Having supreme faith is the cornerstone of a successful and happy life. Everyone has faith whether they like to admit it or not. If you are chronic pessimist, or a realist as some like to describe themselves, then you are putting your faith in the idea that nothing will work out and that big goals are really difficult to achieve. One of the reasons we like to refer to abundance thinking as the "Law" of Attraction is that it helps to solidify the idea in your mind that this is a real phenomenon which holds true and accurate even by empirical standards. The science that we know relies on purely objective and empirical measurements. Because our form of science works and can be tested and shown to be effective, we tend to automatically have faith in it. By referring to something as a law in science, we are in a way hijacking the credibility that science has earned in order to get our message across. The Law of Attraction works every time, in every situation. We can experiment with it and see the results for ourselves. However, the rules of the game are vastly different from the tangible, real-life universe. The universe will manifest results in response to our thought energies however, we must understand that those results may be different than what we expect. For example, let's say you wish for a new car and follow the proper steps to manifest one. A week later, you may be dismayed that your current car was hit in a parking lot and totaled. However, a month later, you find that your insurance company has written off the car, paying you much more than you could have hoped to gain had you chosen to sell it. With this money you are now able to purchase the new car. Out of adversity your goal was realized. Since the universe can work in mysterious ways, it's difficult to approach the Law of Attraction with a traditionally scientific point of view. Instead, you must rely on something inherently unscientific, and that is faith.

It's good that we understand how much of a powerful effect faith has on our lives and that we develop ways to harness it. Many people may feel that if they put their faith in a higher power, they give up their ability to intellectually examine the world. This mode of thinking ends up relying heavily on our sensory inputs and what they tell us about reality. It completely ignores the intangibles or what some philosophers call "universals". These are concepts that exist across all cultures and languages. There exists a noun for the words love, hope, and joy in every language known to man yet we cannot touch or see any of these in an earthly sense. The emotion of love exists yet how can you explain love in terms of science? Of course you can attempt to reduce the emotion to its constituent physical parts and say that it's simply the result of a release of this or that neurotransmitter. Oxytocin doesn't explain the experience of love. No matter how you attempt to break it down and understand love through logic, you will never be able to do so through scientific reasoning. The Germans call this a gestalt — a phenomenon wherein the whole is much greater than the sum of its parts.

Faith is Good for Your Health

Let's look at the scientific research on faith and how it effects our quality of life. There have been numerous valid scientific studies over the years which have shown a significant link to the following positive benefits of faith:

Resiliency is defined as the ability to bounce back from tough problems. A 2004 study published in the American Journal of Psychiatry examined 371 hospitalized patients who exhibited depressive symptoms. The researchers gathered data concerning their depressive episodes throughout their lifetimes including suicide attempts. They found that those who professed a religious affiliation had what they termed a "protective effect" against depression and suicidal ideation. Their results found that *"...religiously unaffiliated subjects had significantly more lifetime suicide attempts and more first-degree relatives who committed suicide than subjects who endorsed a religious affiliation."*

In a more recent 2011 study entitled, Religion and spirituality in Rehabilitation Outcomes among individuals with traumatic brain injury, researchers looked at 88 patients up to 20 years after they had experienced a traumatic brain injury. They found that those patients which professed to have a faith in a higher power scored significantly higher in the areas of well-being, life-satisfaction, emotional distress, and functional ability to navigate the ups and downs of life. They found a directly proportional relationship between faith and a positive recovery.

Evidence of the Law of Attraction in the Bible

When God decided to create the Earth, He did so by first declaring his manifestation through words. *"Let there be Light"* was followed by light. He didn't hesitate, he created. This is manifestation in its most powerful and fundamental form. The bible tells us that we are created in God's image, inferring that also within us lies this awesome ability to create our own lives and manifest our own reality.

Christians should take heart, because the concepts within the Law of Attraction are not incompatible with Christian doctrine or beliefs. Quite the contrary, having faith is a critical part of manifesting your dreams in life. Christianity can act as a powerful vehicle to help you better control your desires and thought energy. Prayer is essentially a targeted and structured approach to asking, the first step in the Law of Attraction. Praising God through song and worship generates positive feelings of joy and helps to keep your mind in an optimum state to create abundance in your life. Attending religious services or participating in rituals such as communion, are powerful methods to maintain and reinforce your faith. All these activities are congruous with elements within the Law of Attraction. The Law of Attraction carries with it no ideology, it simply describes the way in which our consciousness interacts with our physical reality just as the law of gravity describes one aspect of our physical world.

Developing an abundance mentality is not a new phenomenon. Modern teachers of the Law of Attraction sometimes like to market it as some new discovery of which only they have the method to harness it. In reality, the Law of Attraction has been around forever. No person or organization can lay claim to the power of the Law of Attraction. If anyone can, it would be the Christians since the most widely distributed book in the world, the Bible, holds countless examples of the Law of Attraction and your ability as a human to tap into its power.

In the New Testament, Jesus at one point addresses his disciples and says something extraordinarily profound: In Matthew 19:26 he states, *"Humanly speaking, it is impossible. But with God everything is possible."* The mind of man is grounded in the world of his sensory experiences. Only when we move outside of our limited sense of the world, can we achieve anything we desire. With God, we can achieve anything we put our minds to.

The Bible clearly lays out the 3-step process that is the Law of Attraction. In Matthew 21:22, it reads, *"And all things, whatever ye shall ask in prayer, believe, you shall receive it"* This explicitly lays it out for us - we can do, be, or have anything which we desire simply by 1) asking, 2) believing, and 3) receiving.

A big cornerstone of the Law of Attraction is faith. Later in this book we will examine more closely what faith does to our thought energy. Faith is like steroids for your positive thoughts. The second step in the Law of Attraction, believing, is the most important. With true faith, we also lose our worry. By giving up to the universe and letting God worry about the how, we take an enormous burden off our shoulders. The Bible teaches us this also. Psalms 37:4-5 says, *"...Trust in the Lord and he will give you the desires of your heart. Commit everything to the Lord. Trust in him and he will watch over you..."*

I believe the story of Jesus feeding four thousand in the Gospel of Matthew in the New Testament is a symbolic parable in which Jesus is illustrating the power of faith to produce abundance. In the story, Jesus turns a meager amount of food into enough to feed a crowd of four thousand. We call this a miracle, and most would agree that this is impossible for the mere mortal.

"Jesus told the crowd to sit down on the ground. Then he took the seven loaves and the fish, and when he had given thanks, he broke them and gave them to the disciples, and they in turn to the people. They all ate and were satisfied. Afterward the disciples picked up seven basketfuls of broken pieces that were left over. The number of those who ate was four thousand men, besides women and children."

You'll notice here that Jesus first puts himself in a state of abundance by first giving thanks for what he had, albeit a meager amount. His extreme belief allowed him to overcome the limitations of physical reality and produce enough food to feed a massive crowd. From nothing, he created much. Through the power of extreme faith and thankfulness, Jesus was able to tap into incredible abundance.

What Happens When a Person is Born Again

You may have known a person who has experienced a radical spiritual conversion or you may have experienced one yourself at some time in your life. It's truly incredible how a person can be transformed from a lowly depressed state into a successful and respectable individual in a relatively short period of time. Nothing is too strong to overcome and conquer once faith becomes the guiding light in a person's life.

With radical spiritual transformation we can see hardened criminals become caring pillars of the community. We can see drug addicts and alcoholics get sober and lead successful lives. We can see families restored, illnesses healed, and loving relationships restored. There is nothing that cannot be overcome when faith is involved.

If you are an atheist or someone opposed to the idea of faith, try to understand that faith has many real and immediate benefits. We can examine the process of spiritual transformation in others to better our own lives. It's ok to look at faith objectively, but ultimately you will have to give up some of your scientific reasoning and open up your heart and your emotions to something which you might consider scientifically irrational. Let's look at what happens to a person when they go through a radical spiritual conversion — oftentimes referred to as being "born again."

The Four Stages of Radical Conversion

Radical shift in World View - the individual's understanding of their own reality is suddenly filtered through the dogma or ideology of their new belief system. This results in a shift in patterns of thought. Everything now has a purpose and meaning.

Negative Life Circumstances are Reframed - the convert views all their past struggles and heartache throughout their life as a precursor to their conversion event. As a result, they feel gratitude for the trials and tribulations they've experienced. It is weren't for these negative situations and feelings, they never would have come to find their new belief system. Cynicism is replaced by gratitude.

All Worries are given to God - the convert puts their faith in a supreme intelligence or leader who has their best interests at heart. They take action knowing that all things will work for their greater good. This gives the convert the ability to take action knowing that only good things will result from their efforts. If good outcomes are not achieved, the convert falls back to stage 2 and reframes the negative situation as a growing or learning experience.

Maintenance of Belief - the convert is accepted into a social group which reinforces their new beliefs and periodically maintains those beliefs through frequent interaction with others holding the same beliefs such as by attending Sunday church services. Maintenance of faith is necessary because of something known in psychology as cognitive dissonance. The term cognitive dissonance refers to the discomfort we feel when we hold two opposing beliefs. Our minds are predisposed to negative thinking and disbelief. This is a by-product of our evolution. When a convert believes in something that cannot be seen or proven within the realm of empirical reasoning, they will always hold a small doubt in the back of their mind which contradicts their new belief. This is why people can lose their faith. Faith isn't logical and is in direct contrast to the brick and mortar mechanics of reality. By taking periodic action to reinforce a belief, we can strengthen and confirm our faith in the new belief's legitimacy.

It's easy from a scientific perspective, to argue that this sort of conversion process is harmful and misguiding since it tends to lead a person away from the confines of rational thinking. However, when we see the incredible transformative power that the conversion process holds, and how the convert's reality is dramatically transformed to something better, we shouldn't dismiss it. We can examine the conversion process and use it to hack our own beliefs, and therefore radically and quickly change our own reality.

The Law of Attraction is at Work

Religion and dogma are powerful vehicles to fully harness the Law of Attraction. The power that changes the convert's life for the better is the Law of Attraction, not the new dogma or ideology. At the core of every belief system is the Law of Attraction. It's like the active ingredient in a medication. There are many forms of religion, but they all use the same active ingredient to perform miracles in the lives of their converts. Born again believers are generating incredibly powerful thought energies and doing so with enormous faith. The universe responds instantly to this and radical changes will occur. Faith opens doors, while pessimism and doubt closes them.

Using the Conversion Process as Powerful Model for Abundance

So, how can we use the time-tested, centuries old process of religious conversion to hack our own beliefs and generate powerfully positive thought energy that will bring enormous good into our lives? Let's examine each of the 4 stages of religious conversion and see how we can glean the active ingredient, which is the Law of Attraction, from each.

Step 1: A Radical Shift in World View

Start to think of your life as completely within your control. Everything that you have currently is the direct result of your prior thoughts and beliefs. To hack our beliefs and make the Law of

Attraction work as effectively as possible, we need to think of this in terms of a law of science — an irrefutable, non-negotiable way of life that governs everything and everyone. Understand, right at this moment, that you have the absolute power to have, be, or do anything that you chose. You can bring any object, person, or situation into your life simply by applying the Law of Attraction. You are in control. Knowing this and believing this completely just as you would believe in the law of gravity in important to inducing a shift in your own world view.

When you are able to hack your world to believe in the Law of Attraction, you are taking ultimate responsibility for yourself and your life circumstances. You are no longer a victim. You are energized and empowered to create the life you want.

Knowing that your reality is completely your creation and completely within your control causes a radical shift in world view for most people. We must operate from this mindset with all that we do. Take responsibility for your own reality. Accept now that you are the only one who has brought the people, places, and things into your life that you are currently experiencing.

Step 2: Reframe Negative Life Experiences

When something bad happens, it's almost always something that you can reframe into something positive. Adversity brings opportunity. Hardship builds resilience and power. There are of course really bad things that can happen to us such as the death of a loved one. Even with these big things, we can choose to look at the event through the lens of positivity. If our Grandma dies of old age, we can choose to celebrate the long and wonderful life that she lived and the legacy of children and grandchildren that she left behind. We can always reframe a negative into a positive.

Even in trivial things, our initial approach might be to steer things towards the negative. A few years ago I was abruptly reminded of my own tendency to view things through a negative, or as some like to say, *realistic* lens. I went skiing with a friend in the Austrian Alps. I drove my car from my home in Germany to the ski area in Northern Austria. This was very early in the ski season so there was not yet snow on the ground at the lower altitudes. In fact, I had not felt the need to switch from my slick summer tires to my winter tires. In Germany, it's a law that after a certain date, everyone must swap out their summer tires for winter tires, which are capable of driving on snow and ice. We parked the car at the base of the gondola station which was around 4,000 feet (1200 meters). It was a beautiful sunny day and the grass was green and the flowers were still blooming. We took the gondola up and skied all day for about 8 hours on the glacier. At the end of the day, as we rode the last gondola down, I was horrified to discover that a massive snow storm had moved in quickly at the lower altitudes and dumped about 4 feet (1.25 meters) of snow. Needless to say, my car was completely snowed in. With the temperature dropping and the sun setting, we set to work digging the car out.

As I attempted to dig my car out, I allowed worry, anxiety, and a bad attitude to overtake me. I worried about how we would get off the mountain and feared that we would be stuck there throughout the cold and dark night. I envisioned having to call an expensive tow truck and missing work the following day. The worst scenarios started popping into my head.

In contrast, my friend could not stop laughing. He set about helping me dig the car out and just laughed his ass off the whole time. It seemed that he could care less about the situation. A couple of Austrian girls walked by and he even recruited them to help dig us out. His laughter and good spirits were contagious, which caused the girls to also be in a good mood. We ended up cranking up the stereo and the four of us dug the entire car out of the snow as we listened to music. After that, the girls volunteered to drive us down the mountain to purchase some chains.

We found a set of chains at a gas station that fit my car for a reasonable price. The chains worked great, and we were able to get off the mountain safely. We left our new friends laughing and smiling, and even maintained contact with them through social media and went skiing with them a few times later in the season.

This small event caused a huge epiphany to occur within me. How could my pessimism be in such direct contrast with my friend's attitude? Was my view of the events —- being snowed in and trapped on the mountain, more accurate that his view?

Although we both were accurate in the way in which we viewed the event, we differed radically in the way we processed it. He viewed the event through a filter of extreme optimism, while I was focusing on all the things that could go wrong. He had faith that it would all work out. My friend's optimism turned a potential catastrophe into something fun. His approach to the problem cleared away the stress, attracted new friends, and turned it into something humorous. The filter through which we choose to process reality determines our mental state. Our mental state determines whether or not we are generating positive thoughts. Our thoughts create our reality.

Step 3. Give all Worries to God/ the Universe

A huge part of the way that born-agains tap into the power of the Law of Attraction is by completely putting their faith in God that everything will work out in favor of their own goodwill. They trust that God will solve all their problems and that any future struggle that they face will be the direct work of a benevolent God who has engineered a divine purpose for their life.

We can mimic this state simply by having a cool, calm, attitude and unshakeable belief that the universe will deliver good things. There's no need to continually ask the universe for something. Once you've made your request, you can sit back with a renewed sense of confidence knowing that your desire is on its way.

The truth is that every action you take, every person you meet, and every situation you find yourself in is brought to you from the divine. Once you give your desires over to the universe with faith that they are on their way, you will find that events conspire to manifest what you want in your life. The old cliché that everything happens for a reason holds true. This world isn't about random chance - it's about spiritual growth and putting faith in something outside of your own abilities. The universe is an all-powerful force that works in lockstep with your mind to create your reality. It obeys the commands you give it through your thought energies. Have absolute faith that your desires are on their way and they will be.

There's an enormous relief that comes over your when you are able to lay your problems before God (or whatever you choose to refer to your higher power as). Knowing in our hearts that the universe will conspire to achieve our greater good in all situations is incredibly empowering and generates hope. Suddenly, situations which used to worry us and keep us up at night take on an entirely new meaning when we let go of our attempts to control them. Your job is simply to ask and have faith. Let the universe handle the details.

Step 4. Maintaining your Faith

There is somewhat of a myth surrounding religious people regarding faith in that most people assume that once a person has undergone a conversion experience, they are converted for life and will be fueled by a bottomless reservoir of faith. Being the logically-minded human beings that we are, we tend to fall back towards more empirical lines of reasoning after a while. In other words, we tend not to believe in things that we cannot see, feel or hear. If it's outside of the realm of our everyday experiences, and outside the realm of our sensory perceptions, we logically believe things to *not* be true. Why do you think that Christians meet every Sunday? Why do Muslims pray to Mecca five times in a day? These periodic acts of faith serve to reinforce and renew the person's faith. By performing activities or surrounding yourself with the influence of a particular belief system, you can fight your mind's natural tendency for disbelief. Going to church every Sunday can serve to hammer in that nail of doubt that arises when we turn toward deceptively rational thinking.

So how can we emulate the effect of weekly church attendance in order to keep our faith strong and thereby continuously create positive mental energy? We can accomplish this by establishing routines — periodic exercises of faith that will serve to keep us creating thought energy that will manifest big results in our lives.

Examples of Periodic Faith Renewal

- Give thanks every morning (Daily)

- Read a list of Affirmations ex: "I am so grateful and joyous now that..." (Weekly)

- Read books on Positive thinking and the Law of Attraction (Bi-Weekly)

- Visit Law of Attraction websites and blogs (Daily)

- Watch uplifting programs and comedies on TV

- Meditate for 20 mins (1-2 times Daily)

There are many more examples which might apply specifically to your life. For example, if your desire is to become a world-class artist, it would definitely be a good idea to paint or draw daily. If you want to be a great soccer player, practice every day. When we view these actions through the lens of an abundance mentality, they become periodic faith-building routines. Don't worry too much about what that first painting looks like or how well you can juggle a soccer ball — just show up and do it! Be fully engaged in your dream, not worried about the outcome or your current state. Act with faith that your desire will be achieved.

Your Intensity of Faith Determines how Quickly Desires Manifest

The stronger you believe that the Law of Attraction will work for you, the sooner you will see your goals manifest. Time is not a big deal to the universe and you will find that people and situations will rearrange themselves to come into line with the thought energy that you are generating. Our goal is to train our minds to generate only that thought energy which is beneficial to the realization of our desires.

When you believe wholeheartedly that your goal is on its way, you are sending out powerful vibrational energy into the universe. It is important that you feel deeply that you already have your desire. Using a technique called visualization, we can experience now what will manifest in our future. Visualization is the most powerful technique we have for creating positive vibrational energy.

Thoughts Create Vibrational Energy

The vibrational energy that thoughts create can be received by other conscious minds as well as the universal conscious mind that we might call 'God' or simply 'the Universe.' This idea is not a novel concept. Buddhists call it meditation, Christians refer to this practice as prayer, and pagans may call this simply 'ritual'. All these are acts of thought-energy creation. Human beings have been attempting to generate positive thought energy for thousands of years through various methods such as prayer and meditation. The Law of Attraction is the reduction of these methods to a more understandable and verifiable form.

When another conscious mind receives our thought energy, it works to generate thoughts and actions that are congruent with that energy. So too, does the universe as a whole strive for congruence with your thoughts. This process is not one-way. Your mind will receive energy back from the universe and from other minds that conform to your own thoughts. When there is incongruence, the universe and other minds will strive to correct things. For example, if you strongly feel that you will soon receive a large sum of money, and you allow yourself to fully visualize this along with the ensuing emotions, you will be generating thought energy that contradicts your current reality. Sensing an incongruence between your thought energy and your current reality, the universe will then respond by aligning circumstances or people so that you *will* receive a large sum of money, thereby establishing a congruent state.

Whether you Think You Can or Can't, You are Correct

You might ask yourself then, "If things are this easy, why isn't everyone rich and happy?" Well, people are programmed for disbelief from childhood. Skepticism and reliance on our sensory inputs as the only source of "true" information has resulted in an extremely restrained method of thinking about the world. Our negative and limiting beliefs about the world and ourselves causes us to constantly generate negative vibrational thought-energy to the universe. Henry Ford said it best when he stated, "Whether you think you can or you can't, you are correct."

The Doctor Knows Best

Beliefs that are constant and deeply ingrained begin to color all the thought energy that we generate. On the extreme end of the spectrum, we see conditions and diseases such as depression manifest when a person's mind-bias is constantly causing them to generate negative thought energy. As they generate negative thought energy, more negativity and negative situations surface in their lives. This becomes a negative feedback loop that must be broken through therapeutic means. If you are reading this and are experiencing depression, please do not hesitate to seek professional medical help. There are mental states from which a person may be so far in the negative that they cannot pull themselves out without the help of others. Asking for and receiving help from others can be a wonderful joy that immediately starts to turn your life around. Positive social support, church or other spiritual groups, exercise, and limiting alcohol and other drugs all bring immediate and lasting effects to your mental state and help you to start generating positive thought energy. In some cases, your doctor may prescribe anti-depressants to help restore imbalances in brain chemistry. Use these resources, along with the advice of trusted professionals, to dig yourself out of the pit of depression and jump start your positive thinking.

When we think of disease as a symptom of chronic negative thinking, it reframes our own health and our ability to control our physical destiny. Everyone dies, but many chronic diseases are completely avoidable. First and foremost, you should follow the advice of your doctor in regards to your diet and lifestyle. However, it's far too often that medical professionals are relying on a pill as a temporary fix for deeper and more chronic problems. Sometimes these problems are within your control through the power of the Law of Attraction. Anxiety, depression, and other mental diseases can be fixed through actively understanding the reasons behind your condition, and taking directed steps to mediate the problem through the power of positive thinking. As stated previously, this advice does not apply to those suffering from mental conditions resulting from a chemical imbalance or lack of the proper neurotransmitters. For the average person who is experiencing melancholy, lethargy, and a lack of motivation for life, simply shifting your world view to one of abundance will cause a drastic and immediate change for the better. Just knowing that someone has the ability to pull themselves out of these mental states is cause for optimistic excitement.

Chapter 11: How to Hack your Beliefs

Lucky for us, we have the ability to hack our internal beliefs about ourselves and the world. The techniques we use to do this are available to you right now. Simply by using the power of your mind, you can begin immediately to hack your beliefs. The primary methods we will use are as follows:

- Visualization

- Repetitive Affirmation

- Sensory Immersion

Visualization

Visualization involves closing your eyes and imagining the sensations associated with the object or person of your desire. Take the time to examine every minute aspect of your situation, object, or person of your desire. For example, if you are seeking to manifest your soul mate into your life, you can spend time imagining that person — imagine their hair color, eyes, facial features, and personality. Envision the two of you doing things together. Take your time and allow yourself to fully experience any emotions that are generated from the visualization. While visualizing, don't project this image in your mind into as a future state. Rather, **experience it as if it were happening right now.**

When I take the time to visualize something, I close my eyes, breathe deeply, and allow myself to construct mentally the image of what I want. I imagine the lighting, the colors, the smells, and every detailed aspect of the scene. As I do this, the positive emotions begin to come about on their own. Our brains don't know the difference between a situation that is mentally constructed and one that comes from our sense data. As we discussed earlier in this book, reality is always a mental construction. Your mind will construct a reality based on sensory perceptions, and in the absence of sense perception, it will use your imagination. When you visualize, you are tricking your mind into experiencing a reality of your own choosing. The emotions associated with that reality are identical to the emotions that you would experience had the reality been constructed from sense data. This means that we have the ability to generate positive emotions associated with our constructed reality at any time we choose.

Make a habit of visualizing a desired situation. At work, periodically take a few minutes to visualize your goals. You can do this anytime you are waiting in line or any other idle periods throughout your day. By constantly visualizing and generating the feelings of having it now, you will bring the object of your desire into your life. Like attract like.

Repetitive Affirmation

The power of repetition is another potent tool in your arsenal that we can use to hack your long-held beliefs. We can see the power of repetitive suggestion in countless propaganda campaigns throughout history. The propaganda posters of WW2 in the United States promoted the idea that America would soon be victorious, and that the country was a strong and capable nation which could swiftly defeat its enemies. These posters, along with radio and television propaganda, created a constant repetitive suggestion within the psyche of the American people. This repetition had the effect of changing beliefs on a wide scale. By the end of the war, the American people believed with an unwavering faith that victory was in sight.

Look for ways that you can start your own propaganda campaign for yourself. If you desire to hold to the belief of, "money comes quickly and effortlessly to me. I am rich.", then you need to continually reinforce this belief by whatever means possible. Saying affirmations aloud each morning, owning an expensive watch and suit, becoming a member of a country club where wealthy people play golf, these are all ways in which you can reinforce this belief. You've heard the cliche, "fake it until you make it." There's a lot of truth in this. Faking it a great way to create the feelings of having it now. Don't be concerned that physical reality isn't matching up with the mental feelings and beliefs that you've generated. On the surface, this might sound like wishful thinking and honestly a bit insane. When you understand how the Law of Attraction works, you will view this advice through a lens of abundance. When you think abundantly, abundance manifests into your life. By faking it until you make it, you are creating an incongruence that the universe will work to adjust in your favor. If you repetitively affirm that you are filthy rich, yet you have very little in your bank account that is an incongruent state between your beliefs and your physical reality. The mind has the power to overcome physical reality! You must be patient. Consistently and repetitively apply a campaign of personal propaganda. As your beliefs become more ingrained and deepen, the incongruence will become wider and wider until the universe is busting at the seams to establish a balance. In other words, the universe will set up a situation in which you will become filthy rich. This can happen over the course of years or it can happen in the blink of an eye. There are ways however, in which you can control the speed at which the universe adjusts the incongruence in your favor. We will discuss the mechanisms for hacking the speed of manifestation in the next chapter.

Sensory Immersion

Sensory Immersion is an incredibly powerful method we can use to hack our beliefs. This is like visualization on steroids because you will actually seek out situations and people where you can feel now what it is like to have the object or person of desire in your life. This means that you will actually put yourself in a situation where your physical body can sense in real time what the feelings associated with your desire brings. For example, if you are asking for a new car, go to the dealership and test drive that car. While you are test driving the car, use visualization techniques to imagine that you own it *now*. Do not focus on the idea that you are test driving it. Rather, get comfortable in it, imagine that you are driving to work, school, or picking up a friend. This is your car! You already own it! Using this visualization technique, along with the fact that you are actually experiencing the physical touch of the seats, the steering wheel, and the smell of the new car, creates an insanely powerful vibrational energy that tells the universe: "This is my car." Because you found a way to fully immerse yourself in the experience, and your visualization was coupled with the sensations of physical touch and sensory perception, you are able to amplify your vibrational energy beyond what you could do through mental exercises alone.

You can use sensory immersion to bring people of desire into your life as well. Let's say that you desire to date a successful, wealthy business man who is incredibly handsome and caring. Find a situation where you will be in physical proximity to this type of person. Perhaps you can attend a charity event where the men wear tuxes and the women wear elegant evening gowns. If you see someone at this type of event, try to interact with them through conversation over drinks. If not, just being in their presence as they give a speech for example, will generate the sensory inputs that you want for immersion. Imagine yourself being with this person. Imagine yourself in a long term relationship, marriage, kids - whatever your goals are — just imagine everything and anything that creates the vibrational thought-energy which screams to the universe: "This person is my significant other now."

When using sensory immersion to attract people into our lives, we must act appropriately and morally. The process of sensory immersion occurs solely in your mind, so no one needs to know what you are doing. Do not tell anyone that your goal is to generate these thoughts. If you were to disclose to someone that you were imagining what it feels like now to be married to them, they will probably think you are off your rocker. Keep this to yourself, but do understand the process. Always respect others and their space. Using this technique with people is not an excuse to act like a stalker or to inappropriately pursue someone. Show respect and that is what you will receive in return.

"I Am" Statements

A great way to fortify your faith that the universe has placed an order for your desire and that it's on its way is to use powerful "I am" statements. For example, you wished for a new boat, you could say, "I am so happy and grateful now that I can drive my boat every weekend with my kids and wife." As you say these powerful statements, focus on truly believing what you are saying. Don't concern yourself with the fact that it hasn't manifested into your physical reality yet. Remember, we are creating an incongruence between the reality of your mind and the reality of the external physical world. Your mind is incredibly powerful as a tool of creation. When you generate the feelings of having it now, it *will* manifest, every time. **The universe yearns for congruency.** When physical reality is incongruent with your mental vibrational energy, the universe will bend over backwards to fix the discrepancy. When you use "I am" statements, you create a huge rift in the peaceful equilibrium of the universe. Combine this with unwavering faith and you will see fast results, as the universe goes into overdrive to restore the peace. Just like when you throw a rock into a pond and observe the concentric ring of ripples, you see the slow attenuation of those ripples until finally the surface of the water is once again mirror-like and calm. In this same way the universe works to bring calm and peace to incongruences between your mind and physical reality.

I have personally used "I am" statements to become a competitive soccer player. I did not play soccer as a child, and had very little exposure to the sport until the age of 35 when a friend invited me to play one day after work. His team was low on players and they were risking a match forfeiture if they were not able to bring at least 10 players onto the field. My friend knew that I was an avid runner, and so he thought that I might be able to sub in for his C level competitive men's soccer team. Well, to make a long story short, I showed up and played that day, and it wasn't pretty.

I really enjoyed the game however, and I made a commitment to improve. Luckily, his team was consistently short on players that season and they allowed me to sub in every week, despite being the worst player on the pitch. By the end of the season, I had improved enough that they asked me to play with them full time the following season.

After the next season, the team coach decided he wanted to be more competitive, and having access to more players at the time, he cut me from the team. I didn't allow this to put the brakes on my goal of becoming a competitive soccer player though. Being that I didn't have the skills necessary to be selected for a team, I decided instead to start my own team. I put an add out in an online classified system requesting players. The response I received was huge. I was able to call and select the players I wanted. I asked a friend who was good with graphic design to draw up a logo for us, and I ordered 18 full kits so that we could look like a legitimate team. At our first practice, I announced to the team that although I was the team captain, I was going to be the least skilled player on the team. I explained to them how I had been cut from another team, had never played soccer in my life until that year, and how I was looking to build a team and grow and learn from the group. Everyone was a bit stunned by that but they also respected me for having the guts to follow my goal. Every single player got behind me and helped me to improve. We ended up playing together for over three years until I moved to Europe. We actually played the team who had cut me in an indoor championship and beat them 3-2 later that season! After three years with my team, I was able to score goals consistently and handle and pass the ball with decent skill.

During that three year journey, I constantly would use "I am" statements to reinforce my belief in myself. While driving to a match, I would say aloud in my car "I am a consistent goal scorer", "*I am a team player*", and "*I intuitively know when to pass the ball*". The constant repetition of these "I am" statements helped me to solidify the belief that I was a skilled soccer player. It took some time, but my goal was manifested. For someone to start playing soccer at the age of 35 and be able to develop skills of a C level player would be to some an impossible goal. I didn't worry about how it would happen. Instead, I left that part up to the universe to figure out. I simply asked, believed, followed directed and inspired action, and ultimately accepted (received) my desire.

How Fast can it Happen?

Some might ask how fast a belief can manifest into your life. There are several factors at work which determine the speed at which a desire will manifest into your life. First, we must look at the complexity of the request you are sending to the universe. For example, if you ask the universe to become and astronaut and to step foot on Mars, that is a very complex request. This particular request is complex because it requires many things to come into place in order to make this happen. You would need the proper technologies to be developed, as well as the monetary backing and the luck and skill to be chosen for a future mission to Mars. Does that mean it's not achievable? Of course not. Once you start to generate the feelings of being part of an expedition team to Mars, the universe will immediately start to move things around in favor of your desire. However, the universe may have to move a ton of things around in order to make this happen. That means the manifestation could take many, many years.

Fear not though, because there are several other conditions which regulate the speed at which manifestation occurs. The second factor is unwavering faith. The stronger you believe that the object or person of your desire is on its way, the quicker you will see it appear in your life. Developing the feelings of having it now, along with using "I am" statements, will act as a time multiplier to propel you toward the realization of your goals.

The third factor which determines the speed at which a desire is manifested into your life is directed and inspired action. For complex requests, this is arguably the most important factor when it comes to time. Through directed action, we can greatly speed up the process. Through inspired action, we can jump-start or shortcut years from the process. Inspired action is when you suddenly feel the urge to act toward your goal. This is a gift from the universe. Inspired action will be felt as a gentle nudge to move. You may sense a pause or feel some sense of significance emotionally when presented with the possibility of acting in some way. This may come from almost any source — an article in the newspaper, an ad in the back of a magazine, or a person whom you had a chance conversation with on the bus. If you tune yourself to be ready to receive the subtle hints from the universe to act, you will be amazed by the ways which it can radically transform your life.

When I was just out of college, working my first entry level job from a major Internet service provider, I was at the time feeling very disenchanted about my social situation. Specifically, I felt that the group of friends I had in my extended social network were not very supportive and in fact oftentimes were a huge negative influence in my life. I recognized that this was my current condition and that it could be changed. I was at the time new to the Law of Attraction, so I had not yet developed all the skills I needed to manifest things quickly. I sat down in my kitchen one day and wrote the following statement on a piece of paper: *"I am so grateful and happy now that I have a very large group of loyal, fun, exciting, and highly supportive friends who greatly care about me and actively want me to be a part of their lives."* That same night, I received a text out of the blue from an acquaintance I had met about a month prior at a home-brew club meeting. The text was an invitation to hang out at a local festival that was going on in town. Normally, I would likely have ignored the text as I didn't know this person at all. Holding my phone in my hand, I felt a nudge, a gentle urge that said *"go!"* To make a long story short, I went and hung out that night, was introduced to my future girlfriend, and an entire social network of people whom I am very close with nearly five years later. That one event of inspired action was a gift from the universe. The universe was offering a shortcut to manifestation. I had created an incongruent state by firmly asking with an "I am" statement, and then feeling as if it already had happened. Tune your mind to be open to receive the nudges and subtle hints the universe hands you. This will be your quickest way to the manifestation of your goals, especially those goals/desires which are more complex in nature.

To summarize the factors that determine the speed at which the universe will manifest the object or person of desire into your life:

- Complexity of the Request

- Potency of your Unwavering Faith

- Action - Directed and Inspired (especially inspired)

EXERCISE 5

Pick something you wish to manifest as soon as possible. This should be something that you are truly excited and happy about.

- During a meditation session, practice visualizing the object of your desire. Be as detailed and complete as possible, and embrace all positive feelings that arise.

- Each morning, repeat a written affirmation along the lines of *"I am so happy and grateful now that X is in my life."* This only works if you allow yourself to truly *feel* the feelings of gratitude as if you currently possess your desired object or person.

- Repeat Steps 1 and 2 but this time include some form of sensory immersion. For example, if you are wishing to manifest a motorcycle, practice the visualization exercise while sitting in front of a fan, imagining that you are cruising down the road on your brand new motorcycle. Better yet, visit a motorcycle dealership and ask to sit on the motorcycle or take it for a test drive. Imagine that you already own the motorcycle. Allowing yourself to deeply feel the emotions associated with owning the motorcycle.

CHAPTER 12: IDENTIFYING NEGATIVE BELIEFS

Since beliefs arise from persistent thoughts, we need to ensure that our thoughts are usually positive. Our thoughts are strongly influenced by the people, places, and information that we allow ourselves to be surrounded by. Some of those negative influences may be temporarily out of our control. For example, if you have a negative coworker, you may not be able to avoid this person. In cases such as this, it's important to reframe your subjective experience by highlighting the good and minimizing the bad. Adversity is a gift which can result in personal growth and understanding.

The Negativity Bombs

There's a core negativity bomb that you need to be aware of. This type of negativity is so intense that it has the power to destroy much of your positive thoughts and energies. It will actively work in your disfavor. This negativity bomb is **anger**.

Anger is the second most destructive of our emotions. From anger, the most destructive emotion, **hate**, can arise. Hate is something that dissolves in the presence of **love**, and thus we must immediately work to surround ourselves with love. Later in this book, we will address hate, and I will show you a simple exercise that will completely eliminate hate from your life.

Through the practice of a special form of meditation which the Buddhists refer to as "loving-kindness", we can clear hate from our minds and bodies.

Anger is undoubtedly your worst enemy. It is critical that you learn to control your anger. There are many techniques for this but the most effective is simply practicing meditation on a daily basis. When we meditate daily, the ego has less control over us. Anger is an ego-driven emotion. There's no guarantee that you forever be free of it, however, once you have accepted and controlled your egoic mind through meditative practice, you will begin to feel pity and sympathy for others who previously used to anger you. Because your sense of self will be far less dependent upon external opinions, you will not place much value of their behavior or words in relation to your true self. Not caring about the opinions of others allows us simply to observe, understand, and accept rather than process their behavior as a direct assault on our egos.

What happens to you when you are able to resist anger? Others take notice. When we lose our temper, we lose respect. People respect others who can control their emotions. People listen to and follow those people who have a clear, unshakeable belief and understanding of themselves that is not easily swayed by the opinions and emotional attacks of others.

You will likely still have situations where you experience anger. When this happens it's important to breathe and observe non-judgmentally. Accept all emotions. Fully feel and accept them, observing them as something external to your mind and body. They have nothing to do with your social status or the true person you are. Acting on and expressing anger comes from a lack of spiritual maturity. Think back on the last year when you may have lost your temper and done or said something that was harmful to yourself or a loved one. Never act or speak when angry. Always process your emotions first. After you have come to observe and accept anger and you are at peace, then you are in a right position to act.

You may objectively conclude the person who angered you is a real source of negative energy or they may genuinely have a malicious nature. In this case, you can calmly eliminate them from your life without drama. You may also find that the actions or words which angered you are valuable in that they were an accurate assessment of some aspect of your being. You can use this as a catalyst for positive change and in many cases your feelings will shift to those of gratitude for this person. In the case of the person whom you find to be genuinely malicious, it is possible also to form a sense of gratitude for that person because they taught you an incredibly valuable lesson to avoid similar people or situations in the future.

The Dangers of Rumination

Rumination is simply the compulsive focus on negative thoughts and images. Usually this is one of the central causes of depression. Oftentimes, rumination occurs subtly and under the surface. We may not even realize that we are ruminating. If you wake up and think about how your job sucks, you'll carry that attitude throughout the day and, guess what? — Your job will probably suck. Conversely, if you wake up and say thank you to the universe for having a job, you'll carry an attitude of gratitude with you throughout the day. Gratitude destroys rumination.

Rumination deserves special focus because it can be such a hindrance to the manifestation of our desires. It can follow us throughout the day and tilt our thinking towards a highly negative frame. We tend to ruminate about past, current, and future events. For past events, we might recall a time in which we felt slighted and disrespected. Rather than blowing it off and not placing value on the perceived slight, we might ruminate on it and let it continue to build negative feelings of mistrust and hatred. Instead of viewing it as an isolated event, we build it up and allow it to colour our perceptions of reality. Every day, we will encounter something which has the potential to upset us, threaten our ego, or just make us sad in general. It's the significance that we give these events, and the way we think about them that is important. If we allow them to continuously circle in our mind, we start to develop a bad attitude about the world and other people. It's a normal tendency for us to place emphasis on negative actions and thoughts over positive ones. This is part of our evolution. In order to survive, we had to be aware of any and all potential threats. Therefore, our minds are on constant alert as to potential enemies and situations which could harm us.

Negative emotional experiences have a high survival value. You are more likely to stay alive, from an evolutionary perspective, when you ruminate on negative things. Your brain wants to churn though thoughts, and dwell on the most negative things over and over, in an effort to understand potential threats. This can wreak havoc on our state of mind, happiness, and ability to generate the positive thought-energy required for manifestation.

Embrace All Your Emotions

So, knowing that we are a bit screwed evolutionarily and are predisposed to negative thinking, how can we work to overcome this tendency? Well, we could try a strong arm approach and force ourselves to constantly monitor and adjust our thinking but this is fatiguing and not sustainable over the long term. The key to taking the power out of negative thoughts is to change the way you judge those thoughts. First, accepts negative thoughts rather than attempting to push them away. Lots of emotions are overwhelming and that's the primary reason that people turn to things like drugs, alcohol, and even sex. There's a huge list of diversions out there that take our mind off of our problems. Lots of these are ok in moderation. TV watching for example, can be an escape from negative thinking. Watching a funny sitcom can actually help to put us into a happy mood. If we start to live vicariously through a television series or we find that TV becomes our main activity outside of work, then we've entered dangerous territory. When we turn to something in order to avoid our negative emotions, we're no longer really living. The correct solution is to embrace all your emotions. Allow yourself to feel the pain. Get comfortable with it.

Spiritual leader and author, Eckhart Tolle, refers to the negative emotions we carry with us as the "pain body". I have never seen a better explanation as to the processes and reasons for negative emotions than from Eckhart. I highly recommend his book, A New Earth. It was one of the first books I read on my journey of spiritual health and I credit his teaching to much of my current success today.

The pain body will always be with us. What causes us pain is not the negative emotions themselves, but rather our identification with them. In other words, we will associate our own sense of self with these negative emotions. Each time that you experience a negative event, a negative emotion is generated, leaving behind a residue of pain. Your life becomes defined by a string of emotional pains that linger for years. Substances, time, and/ or diversions can distract your mind from the growing pain body, but it will always be there.

Think of your pain body as something physical. You can't see it but it actually surrounds your physical being. In a normal person, your pain body lies dormant most of the time. As soon as you experience a negative situation though, that person's pain body wakes up, and starts to take control. This explains why a simple comment or slight can throw someone into a depression or even into an angry rage. Think of the pain body as a parasitic cloud that surrounds your body, sapping your strength and destroying your peace of mind. The pain body wants your mind to directly reflect its own negative state. This means that it wants your mind to experience what it is - pure pain. The pain body wants to survive. It will do anything it can to survive. Its survival depends wholly on your ability to identify with it. It draws its energy from controlling your thinking and aligning itself with your thoughts.

Rumination is essentially the result of your pain body attempting to take complete control of your thinking in order to ensure its survival. The pain we experience comes when our egos identify with the pain body. The idea that your pain body defines you is a falsehood that your pain body wants you to believe.

The good news is that there's an extremely simple way to dissolve the pain body and the pain that it brings. Observe it. Simply by observing the pain body as an external entity made up of an accumulation of your life's painful moments, you will consciously take away its power. The pain body is an identification with the past. The past has no power over you now or in the future. Just because we failed yesterday, or failed 1000 times over decades, doesn't mean that we will fail tomorrow. The act of observing your pain body automatically results in a misidentification with it. This will dissolve the pain. You can also use the Green Blob Method discussed in Chapter 3 to help visualize the pain body as something external to yourself.

You'll need to constantly be aware of the pain body's presence since it will continuously attempt to spring back to life and control your thinking. A very effective way to do this is with mindfulness meditation. A simple meditation, where we sit quietly and observe the pain body as something external from ourselves; completely separate from our identity; is a very powerful way to disassociate from it.

CHAPTER 13: DANGEROUS DIVERSIONS

Sometimes when we ruminate, we feel a strong desire to escape the perception of pain that our pain-body activates. For most people, the easiest response to emotional and physical pain is avoidance. We accomplish this through what I call **dangerous diversions**. This can be drugs, alcohol, sex, obsessive TV or movie watching, or video games. Watching TV can be a nice diversion at times, but if you find yourself rushing home from work only to pop open a beer and watch TV all night, then you might have a problem. Why are these diversions potentially harmful? Because they take us out of reality. Rather than confronting the cold hard truth of our current state, we are choosing to stick our heads in the sand and avoid present conditions.

With dangerous diversions, we cannot make positive changes. Experts say that alcoholics stop maturing emotionally at a young age. Their chronic drinking stunts their ability to understand others and their own place in the world. Dangerous diversions of *any* type cause us to stop growing and learning because they shield us from our own raw emotions.

Emotions are critically important because they are the mind's way to tell us that something is potentially wrong. Positive emotions also tell us when we are on the right track. Negative emotions are your mind's way to prompt you to action. If you are suppressing or avoiding negative emotions through the use of dangerous diversions, you will never take the action needed to resolve your problems.

When someone chronically uses dangerous diversions to avoid potentially painful emotions, they become emotionally immature. It's good to know what the signs of emotional immaturity are so that you can recognize them in yourself and others. Emotionally immature individuals tend to:

- Have difficulty dealing with the normal challenges of life

- Feel helpless to change, feel victimized by life

- Have low self-esteem

- Find it very hard to live in the present moment

- Hold unrealistically high expectations for themselves and others

- Suffer from severe mood swings

- Have difficulty dealing with other people

If you see some signs of emotional immaturity in yourself, be glad that you've identified them. It doesn't take long, once you've made some changes and eliminated your dangerous diversions, to start seeing the return of your emotional growth. Our brains are incredibly resilient, and if we treat ourselves right, our minds will reward us.

Alcohol and Drugs: The Emperor's New Clothes

We've all heard the story of the emperor's new clothes where the clueless emperor is caught up in the glamour and prestige associated with a set of exotic clothes which only those of high intelligence who are fit for their post can actually see. There are many commentaries as to the meaning of this story but I interpret it like this: There are many things in life that appear to be beneficial by popular belief, but the majority of people are too caught up in what everyone else is thinking or how they are supposed to think that they ignore the truth in front of them.

Just because alcohol has become a normal part of the human experience doesn't mean that it's beneficial for you. In moderate amounts alcohol is harmless, yet binge drinking has become the norm among many people throughout the world. The UK's National Health Service just drastically lowered their recommended allowances for alcohol intake and other medical organizations have started to examine the status quo as well. Just because lots of people act or believe a certain way doesn't mean it's correct or healthy.

Alcohol and other drugs make us less conscious; less in tune with our emotions and reduce our ability to grow spiritually. Even what many consider normal drinking patterns can have significant effects on our executive decision making skills, and our ability to empathize and connect on a real level with others. The longer we practice abstinence and freedom from intoxicating substances, the stronger our ability to generate strong vibrational energy and feelings. In other words, clouding your brain with alcohol and drugs drains your spiritual energy. Intoxication clouds and distorts your ability to generate the positive feelings of abundance and self-worth needed to manifest the object or person of your desire.

EXERCISE 6

On a sheet of paper, make a list of six dangerous diversions that you practice. Anything that pulls you out of reality and suppresses your painful emotions is potentially a dangerous diversion. People tend to get caught in the trap of thinking that a dangerous diversion is anything that is labelled as potentially harmful. Excessive exercise can be a dangerous diversion. Anything that results in you metaphorically sticking your head in the sand is potentially damaging. Look at your list of your six dangerous diversions. Identity the two most damaging diversions and circle them. Make a plan to completely eliminate these two. Start today or tomorrow, but write a date next to each one and commit to completely stopping this activity on that date. For the remaining four diversions, assess to what degree each of these causes you to suppress or avoid your emotions. Make a plan to either eliminate these or severely limit them in your life. Next to each, write your plan to eliminate or limit each one. For example, if you watch TV every day, make a commitment to cut that down to 2-3 days a week. You'll find that you end up with a lot of time on your hands to engage in actually living life. I've done this exercise many times throughout my life, and you may find yourself sitting at home, staring at your dog, cat, or significant other and thinking, "OK what do I do now"? Never fear, there's an answer to that question and it's what I call **activities of conscious engagement** or **ACE**.

CHAPTER 14: ACE - ACTIVITIES OF CONSCIOUS ENGAGEMENT

"Don't count the days, make the days count." – Muhammad Ali

I once worked in the IT department for a very large telecommunications company in the United States. There I met an interesting guy named Bob. Bob was incredibly intelligent and was one of our top engineers. He could consistently solve problems that other couldn't and senior leadership relied on him more than anyone on our team to resolve the toughest of issues. Because Bob was so essential, he survived 14 rounds of layoffs throughout the financial turmoil of the 2000s. Bob didn't have a degree or any industry certifications. He never managed people or sought a management role within the company. Bob was content to sit in his corner cubicle, surrounded by posters of different fantasy characters. He had a life size replica of Darth Vader that stood like a guard over his domain, and his desk was covered with action figures, robots, and gizmos of every sort. Not only could Bob solve any problem involving a computer, he could also quote every line from every fantasy or sci-fi movie ever made.

Bob made a great salary. As others were laid off around him over the years, management knew that it was important to keep Bob around, because he could fix the big problems that came their way. When a major US bank who used their data service experienced an outage costing them millions of dollars for every minute they were down, Bob could step in and save the day on most occasions. As a result, Bob received huge pay raises and yearly bonuses.

Bob paid off his house, car and motorcycles with cash, and bought any toy he wanted. By many accounts, lots of people would look at Bob and say that he was highly successful. However, Bob felt empty and lost. In his late 40s, he had never had a girlfriend and never even attempted to ask a girl out. His daily routine consisted of going to work, coming home and watching movies on his huge flat screen with a $20k surround sound system. When he wasn't watching fantasy movies, he was playing video games until the wee hours of the morning. Over the years, Bob neglected his physical health and become more and more overweight. As the years crept by, he became progressively more and more depressed, and he began to drink to ease the pangs of reality. Soon, the movie watching and game playing included large amounts of beer and high dollar Scotch.

Working with Bob for several years and learning about him, I recognized that Bob was in a dangerous cycle. He was anxious about facing life straight on and consciously. To reduce that anxiety, he would escape into his fantasy world of movies and games. The drinking contributed to his anxiety, weight gain, and isolation. As his habits fueled more depression and pain, he attempted to remedy his situation by seeking more and deeper methods of escape.

One day, I asked Bob if he'd like to grab a beer after work. I had an intervention of sorts with him and explained very bluntly and directly what I had observed. I suggested that he start running and back away from the habits which were really an escape mechanism. Living consciously, I explained, took guts and the willingness to risk everything, but the rewards were the real treasure. Because I knew that Bob was analytically minded, I used the analogy of programming to describe what I wanted to say. I told Bob that life was like a game, and that there are a set of rules for success. If you program your life according to those rules of success and abundance, you will have the output you desire, whatever that output might be. The output, I explained, is 100% determined by the lines of code that *you* create for your life.

Bob was quiet for a while after I spoke. His head was hanging low and he stared blankly at the beer in front of him at the bar. He finally looked at me and said, *"You're right. And no one has ever told me what I needed to hear so badly before."*

That same week, Bob started a couch-to-5k program. Several months later, I ran with him in his first 5k. Roughly six months after that, he ran his first half marathon. The weight fell off of him and his self-esteem shot through the roof.

Bob took a break from alcohol, and his anxieties subsided. He joined a local gym and started to go out more. Friends at work and family members started to invite him to parties and BBQs. Everyone discovered that the real Bob had a great personality, and Bob found that he enjoyed being around others.

About a year after Bob made his radical life change, he met a girl at a community festival in the city. He spent several hours with her and they laughed and talked effortlessly. Before she had to leave, he asked for her number and told her that he would like to see her again. She gave him her number, and left him with a kiss on the cheek. Bob was so ecstatic that he called me the next day to tell me the news. I knew that this was a huge step for him so I congratulated him and wished him the best on his date with her. I spoke with him a few weeks later and he told me that he had gone on several dates already with her and that things seemed to be going well. He said that even if things didn't work out with this girl, he would continue to pursue women whom he found interesting. He truly understood that living a conscious life means acting deliberately, taking risks, and filling your life with **activities of conscious engagement**. I like to refer to these as ACE. You'll find that the more you incorporate ACE into your life, the more that living consciously becomes a habit and eventually a lifestyle. Once you experience the incredible joy and excitement of a consciously lived life, you won't want to go back to a life of dangerous diversions.

What exactly is ACE?

Activities of Conscious Engagement are the activities that you were designed for. As spiritual beings, we were made not just to exist in this world, but to thrive. We can only do this when we are taking chances, exploring, engaging with others, and using all our talents. When you take the time to learn something new, be creative, or have a meaningful conversation with another person, you are growing. Any activity where you are fully conscious, present-minded, and learning is ACE. I recently found myself watching documentaries at home after work on nights when I had nothing else going on. On the surface this sounds harmless, but I recognized that this time was a potentially dangerous diversion. Even though I was learning things by watching a documentary, I was using the documentary as an escape to avoid the present moment. I was telling myself that it was OK because it was educational. In reality I was just zoning out. As a solution, I limited my YouTube watching and started a new hobby to fill that time. I bought a sketch book and started drawing. After a few weeks, I started using colored pencils and venturing out of the house to draw on location. My mom is a professional artist, and when she got word that I had started this new hobby, she sent me a small treasure trove of art supplies. From that I tried watercolor painting and fell in love with it. I am by no means a fully developed artist, but I now complete one painting a day and even started my an art blog to document my progress. Several friends have had my paintings matted and framed and hung them in their homes. Recently, I received a request to purchase one the paintings I posted on my blog. Had I not recognized that my documentary watching was a dangerous diversion, I would never have discovered this new way to tap into my creative power.

Some examples of ACE:

- Sports

- Socializing without alcohol

- Painting, Drawing

- Writing

- Being in Nature

- Meditation

- Studying

- Learning a new Language

- Cooking

- Sex

- Cleaning, organizing

- Reading

- Exploring a new city or region

- Road trip with friends

- Prayer

- Physical Labor

- Paying bills, budgeting

- Gratitude exercises

- Volunteering

- Acts of kindness toward your friends or a random stranger

- Setting goals

- Playing a musical instrument

- Teaching

- Taking a class

- Meaningful and honest conversation with someone

There are many more examples of ACE. ACE can be anything in which you are using your talents or building skills with a *fully present mindset*. In other words, anything that doesn't serve to dull or suppress your emotions. You'll find that your mind is fully engaged and that you start to exhibit emotional resiliency the more you practice ACE. You're interactions with others will be more genuine and real, and you will develop a sense of self-assuredness that casts a positive light over your entire life. Replacing dangerous diversions with ACE will radically transform your relationships, peace of mind, and feelings of self-worth.

I've found a great app that I use called Way of Life Journal. It enables you to create daily activities and track whether or not you complete them. I love to use this as a way to stay on track and to ensure that I engage in ACE on a daily basis. In the app, I create daily events for writing, art, meditation, study time, and my TO-DO list. I also track my alcohol intake and my daily exercise. The app has some nice visuals that display your ACEs in 31 day increments. This creates an easy method to see if you are staying on track. If you skip a day for a particular ACE, it's no big deal. More important is that you consciously work to make ACE part of your daily life.

Once you start to eliminate the daily activities and habits that are robbing you of life and emotional maturity, you'll find that you have loads of time to deal with. At first, having nothing to do can be very uncomfortable. It can at times even be painful. I have a friend who obsessively watched television for many years. He lived vicariously through sitcoms such as Friends and That 70s show. Those are funny shows, and it's alright to watch them occasionally, don't get me wrong. My friend however, would often turn down offers to hang out and stay at home watching TV instead. Every so often, he and I would meet for lunch, and he would talk about his various sitcom characters as though they were real people in his life. He had replaced his social life with a fantasy world consisting of a collection of TV characters. In this, he felt no potential for rejection; no potential for pain. After intervening with him, he agreed that he needed to make some changes. I asked him to complete the above exercise and the two dangerous diversions that he agreed to eliminate were watching television and playing guitar hero on his PlayStation. After the first day, he called me because he was bored. He expressed to me that without his sitcoms, he felt lonely. He and I met up for a beer and talked. After a few months, he was actively engaged in social activities and had even made some new friends. Additionally, he started weight training at the gym near his house. He stuck with it, and now even though he still watches TV occasionally, he has a real social life with real friends, and as a result he has grown emotionally. Later that year, he told me he had never felt better mentally or physically in his life. Had he never eliminated his dangerous diversion of obsessive TV watching, he would have remained emotionally stunted. As soon as he cut out the TV watching, he was forced to face his own fears of social rejection and self-imposed isolation. Engaging in ACE, he was able to move forward with his life.

EXERCISE 7

Take out a clean sheet of paper. Write down ten ACE that you can start to do in the next month. Next to each ACE, write out a quick action plan to jumpstart you. For example, if you wrote down "Start drawing again", you might write as your quick action plan, *Buy new sketchbook and pencils tomorrow*. It's important that you include deadlines or dates in your action statement since this will provide a sense of urgency. Keep your list of ten ACE that you'd like to implement in a visible place such as hanging in your office at work next to your computer monitor or on your refrigerator at home.

If you've identified and eliminated enough of your dangerous diversions, you'll have plenty of time to fill. Work daily to fill your time with the ten ACE that you've listed here.

CHAPTER 15: THE GIFT OF ADVERSITY

"Every day, think as you wake up, today I am fortunate to be alive, I have a precious human life, I am not going to waste it. I am going to use all my energies to develop myself, to expand my heart out to others; to achieve enlightenment for the benefit of all beings. I am going to have kind thoughts towards others, I am not going to get angry or think badly about others. I am going to benefit others as much as I can." - The Dalai Lama

I remember as a kid going to Sunday school and learning about Job and his tribulations. If you haven't been exposed to the book of Job, it's basically about a guy who has everything taken from him — his family, friends, wife, money — you name it. The worst part about this story is that all the horrible things that happen to Job are the direct result of God's actions. The devil was talking with God and they made a kind of bet that Job, being a loyal follower of God, would forsake and abandon God if enough bad things happened to him. God decided to test Job and see if the devil was right. As more and more bad things happened to Job, he was eventually left penniless and writhing in misery, but he never lost his faith in God. The moral of the story is that you never really know what God's plans are. Job did not know that his suffering was the result of God's test. When we experience suffering, we do not know all the facts. Unfortunately, the story of Job doesn't really have a happy ending. As a kid, I remember being very disturbed by it. However, we can use it as an example to illustrate a very important point about suffering and adversity: it happens for a reason.

The first reaction you should have to bad news, adversity, or suffering is to give thanks. The universe has set up a customized situation just for you to help you be where you need to be, meet the right person, change your job, or any other opportunity in the list of infinite possibilities. Your suffering is uniquely crafted for your benefit, and it means that God is working in your life.

Potatoes, Eggs, and Coffee

One day, a little girl came home from a rough day at school and complained to her daddy that she hated her life and no longer wanted to go back to school. The father patiently listened to her as she went on and on and how the popular girls at school were gossiping about her, about how the boy she liked ignored her, and about how she felt like she had no friends. She felt that life couldn't get any worse, and at 12 years old, the little girl was ready to throw in the towel. With tears in her eyes, she looked at her father and asked, "Why is life so hard?"

The father was very concerned and took the little girl into the kitchen where he sat her down and told her to pay close attention. The father took out three pots, filled them with water, and sat them on the stove under high heat. When all three pots began to boil, he added potatoes to one, eggs to the second pot, and ground coffee beans to the third. After a while, he removed the potatoes and the eggs, and poured the coffee into a cup.

Turning to his now very impatient daughter, he asked her: "What do you see here honey?"

"Potatoes, Eggs, and coffee." The girl was confused.

"Look closer - what do you *feel* when you touch the potatoes?"

"They're soft daddy"

"That's right." The father smiled.

"Now what do you see when you touch the eggs?"

She took an egg and broke it, observing the soft white of the egg inside.

"Now take a sip of the coffee"

She did so, paused and looked up at him, eyes red from crying. "What's does this mean daddy?"

The father then smiled and explained the meaning to his little girl. All three ingredients faced the exact same adversity — the boiling water. The potatoes went in strong and resistant, but in the boiling water they became soft. The eggs went in with a hard protective outer shell yet it could not protect the inside of the egg from becoming hard in the boiling water. The coffee grounds were different - they responded to the boiling water by transforming into something new. The coffee responded by transforming itself into something even better than it was before.

The father looked at his little girl and asked with a smile, "Which one would you like to be like? The potato, the egg or the coffee?"

The Universe Chooses the Quickest Path

Every single bad thing that happens in your life has the ability to change you for the better. It can make you depressed and cynical, or it can cause you to grow and mature spiritually and emotionally. Discomfort and misery often follow success, because you need to experience some turmoil in order to either learn a lesson or to grow and change as an individual in some way.

Don't be alarmed but sometimes when we ask the universe for something, we may experience some adversity *before* we see our desire manifest. This is because the universe is working to change a situation or to change you so that you can receive the object of your desire. Let me give you an example. Let's say that you are a socially awkward individual who feels uncomfortable in large groups. You might ask the universe to be confident and socially savvy. Well, the universe always uses the quickest approach to manifest your goal. That may not always be the gentlest approach. In this example, you might find yourself suddenly thrown into social situations where you are forced to adapt and respond socially in ways you never have before. Your normal behavior might be to avoid the potential pain of socializing at this level however, if you understand that this is part of the process, you can accept the new stress as something constructive. This is the key — understanding that adversity and suffering are part of a process to make you better, stronger, or smarter in some way. The universe always has your best interest in mind — it will respond to your request immediately and quickly. It does not care if you experience some pain along the way toward the realization of your goals. Just be patient and understand that at the right time, when you've learned what you need to learn, you will see the manifestation of your desire.

Suffering is Part of the Plan

Knowing that suffering is part of the plan means that you view it differently. It takes the sting out it. It helps you to confront it and to fully experience the suffering because you know that it's for your benefit ultimately. Perhaps you have a bad boss or coworker whom you can't avoid? Be thankful for this person in your life, because they are there for a reason. You might discover that you have your own character defects that need to be worked on. Adversity truly is a reason to be happy. There are big problems and situations such as the death of a loved one that seem overwhelming. You might wonder how these things are for your ultimate benefit. Through this level of suffering we learn humility, peace, appreciation for the present, and greater understanding and acceptance of the constant state of change we are in. In everything, there's a human lesson that we are meant to learn.

The ability to reframe negative experiences will have an enormous impact on your life. When you are mired in a negative situation, it can sometimes seem impossible to find the silver lining. Trust me, there is one! Everything *does* happen for a reason, and your adversity is reason to give thanks because the universe is working within you for your positive benefit. Now it's important to understand that the positive benefit only comes when we reframe our thinking. If your response to adversity is to slip into rumination and depression or to develop a cynical attitude, then the universe will respond in kind. It's only when we view adversity as a positive potential that miracles will occur.

Adversity and Resilience are Part of Success

Successful people in life all share the characteristic of resilience, or the ability to bounce back from failure. Additionally, they seek the silver lining in every negative situation. To illustrate this point, and to get you excited about hardship and adversity, let's look at some examples of very successful people who have reframed negative situations to their benefit:

Bill Gates - Did you know that one of the richest men in the world was at one time a failure in business? In 1974 Bill and his business partner Paul Allen, started a company called Traf-O-Data. The company's business plan was to secure contracts with state and local governments to count vehicle traffic. You know those little black tubes you sometimes see on the highway? They built a computer that could count cars every time they drove over the black tubes. Although the plan was sound, and they put hundreds if not thousands of man hours into their demo computer, it turned out to be a total flop. At a demonstration with the State of Washington transportation authorities, their demo machine malfunctioned, and their first big sale was lost. The company never recovered.

Do you think that they let this failure stop them in their pursuit of business success? Bill and Paul both expressed gratitude for the experience, stating that without the failure of this first company, they would never have been prepared for the launch of Microsoft a few years later.

Oprah Winfrey - One of my all-time favorite people, Oprah faced a tumultuous childhood and a tremendous uphill battle toward success. Her early life was riddled with many upsets and failures before achieving super star status as a talk show host and eventually emerging as a spiritual and cultural leader. Growing up poor and in a transient status, she was the victim of physical and sexual abuse as a child.

In her days as a news anchor, she was sexually harassed and eventually was fired from her position. Shortly after, she took an unknown talk show in Chicago and worked hard to eventually turn the little show into what later became "The Oprah Winfrey Show".

Oprah's tribulations have shaped her into the incredibly insightful, humble, and enlightened spirit that she is today. Her personal knowledge of human suffering has enabled her to share an intelligent humanism with the world.

Jim Carey - A truly amazing person and a strong advocate for the Law of Attraction, Jim Carey overcame many failures throughout his life to become the man he is now. The first time that Jim ever stepped on stage for a comedy gig, he was promptly booed off. When he auditioned for Saturday Night Live, he was rejected. Few people know that Jim Carey grew up so poor that he was forced to drop out of High School in order to work and help support his family. The only job he could find was as a low paying janitor. Jim did not allow any of this to stop him in the pursuit of his dreams. Jim Carey wrote himself a check for $10,000,000 dollars and put it in his wallet. He was at that time sending a thought out to the universe and tapping into the power of the Law of Attraction. Within seven years he *did* receive a check for that amount for his role in Dumb and Dumber.

J.K Rowling - It's hard to fathom that one of the world's most successful female authors was at one time facing a series of professional and personal failures. After a short marriage that ended in a bad divorce, she went through periods of depression and poverty. At one point, she lived solely on government welfare. In 1995 she finished the first Harry Potter book, one of her most famous and entertaining books. The manuscript was rejected an unbelievable twelve times before a publisher finally considered publishing it! The first run of Harry Potter was very small and consisted of just 1000 copies. After the book began to receive some exposure and acclaim, its popularity snowballed into an out of control freight train of success. She has currently sold more than 400 million copies within the Harry Potter series.

Thomas Edison - Perhaps no one in history could hold claim quantitatively to the sheer number of failures that Thomas Edison experienced before he achieved success with the electric lightbulb. Edison tried over 10,000 different wicks and compounds before finding a combination that worked. Edison was relieved from two positions for not producing results, and one of his elementary teachers declared that he was "too stupid to learn". He considered his many failures not really failures because they were at least eliminating the things that didn't work. His perseverance and ability to refrain his failures resulted in the invention of the lightbulb, drastically reshaping modern civilisation.

Michael Jordan - The most famous player in basketball world history, winning 6 NBA Championships, 5 MVP trophies, and a dozen all-star games as well as two Olympic gold medals, was once rejected from his university team. At the time, his coaches felt that he needed more time to develop and that he wasn't yet tall enough to compete at the university level. He was instead selected for the university junior team and proceeded to dominate at that level until his talent could no longer be ignored. Michael has repeatedly stated in interviews that he owes all his success to his previous failures, and that they served as the fuel he needed to persevere and become one of the greatest basketball players of all time.

Whenever we are faced with a tough situation, we must learn to recognize the benefits that will come from the hardship. When we change our thinking in this way, endless possibilities open up to us and the world no longer seems like it's out to get us. To the contrary, finding the ability to appreciation adversity in our lives allows us to reframe the adversity as something positive. The universe will respond in kind to your positive frame of reference, and you will see good come from at what first seems negative. Enemies will become friends, poverty turns to riches, and disease turns to health. When we reframe our adversity as something positive, we will always see unlimited abundance in the long run.

Many people might find this concept easy to grasp but difficult to put into practice. When faced with adversity, there are some questions you can ask yourself to help you reframe the experience:

- In what way does this adversity positively affect me?

- What can I learn from this adversity?

- With this adversity, what new opportunity is now possible?

- How will this experience make me stronger, wiser, and more resilient?

• What reasons do I have to be thankful for this situation?

EXERCISE 8

Take out a piece of paper and draw three columns. At the top, label each column left to right as the following: Goal, Limiting Belief, and Abundant Belief. Under the Goal column, list your top ten goals which you wish to manifest *now* into your life. These should be the top ten goals from the ASK chapter that we covered previously. For each goal, pause to reflect on what limiting beliefs you currently hold about that goal. For example, if you wish for a new car, you might have a limiting belief that says "I can't afford it". You can transform that limiting belief into something in-line with the manifestation of that object. For this example, you might state, *"Money comes easily to me. Covering my expenses is easy."* Do this for each of your top ten goals.

Identifying Negative People

"Stop letting people who do so little for you control so much of your mind, feelings and emotions". – *Will Smith*

We cannot control the thought energy of others, nor should we attempt to. You will find that there are people who have chronic ways of thinking which may emanate strong negative energy. Have you ever met someone and just felt an odd sense of disease? Sometimes you may have no objective or apparent reason for disliking someone. Your mind is extremely protective of your mental health. Whenever it senses a threat, real or imagined, it jumps into protective mode. This is a good thing, however, we need to differentiate between what is a legitimate threat and what is just a matter of skewed perception. In extreme cases, such as agoraphobia or extreme introversion, the mind's threat perceptions are highly inaccurate and need to be adjusted in order for the person to function effectively.

Meditation and mindfulness is your greatest tool in strengthening the accuracy of your sense perceptions. By clearing away the clutter of egoic attachments, we can view the world through a much more accurate lens.

CHAPTER 16: REDUCE YOUR EXPECTATIONS OF OTHERS

"I'm not in this world to live up to your expectations and you're not in this world to live up to mine." – BruceLee

Part of understanding, appreciating, and supporting yourself free from the opinions of others is managing your expectations. Humans are fallible and inherently selfish. They will oftentimes say or do things which serve their own interests first. Some people will go to elaborate lengths to convince you that they have your best interests in mind when in reality they are only trying to recruit you as a potential pawn in their ego-boosting strategies. This behavior can be so engrained in a person that they don't even realize that their actions are malicious and harmful.

Knowing that humans have this tendency, it's important that you detach your self-worth from the opinions and actions of others. This does not mean that you should reject *all* criticism. To the contrary, you should embrace and be thankful for criticism in all forms when it's valid and truthful. However, criticism should never diminish your sense of self-worth in any way. Everyone on this earth can improve in some way and is therefore a viable candidate for criticism. Being criticized is a gift when it's valid. You should look at the criticism as something external from who you are - it is an assessment of your behavior — not of you as a person.

Having high expectations of others only sets yourself up for disappointment. It's ok to expect greatness and success from yourself, but don't apply your standard to those around you. Their actions and standards are none of your business unless you are directly responsible for their work in a professional setting. In this case, address the work standard and nothing else. In your personal life, the expectations you place on others should be minimal.

This might seem like odd advice at first, but let's look at some examples. Let's say that you have a friend whom you told a secret to and expressly asked them to keep this secret between the two of you. Not long after, this person discloses your secret and you find out about it. If you're angry and disappointed, it's because this person did not meet the expectation of trust that you held in your mind of them. This isn't their fault. Learn from this situation. Now you know that this person isn't to be trusted. You should not hold any animosity toward them — simply understand that this person views the world differently than you and that the expectation *you* hold for *yourself* does not apply to them.

Never put absolute faith in the words or actions of others. You can know that a person is most likely to be honest, most likely to be a good friend, etc, but you can never *expect* that person to always hold true to these standards. The thoughts, actions, words, and behaviors of others are out of your control. They hold no power over you. Continue to practice excellence in your own life but do not expect excellence from others.

Another example may be the friend who constantly backs out at the last minute on plans. You may find this not only annoying but disrespectful. Don't look at it that way. Their behavior has nothing to do with you. Once you have identified that this person has a tendency to flake, take measures in the future to mitigate the impact their behavior will have on you. For instance, if you invite them on a trip where they would be required to split some costs such as a hotel room, ensure that they pay well in advance of the trip date. This way you and the others in your group will not be economically affected if they choose to back out at the last minute. Don't however, hold any animosity towards this person. Simply accept them as they are and appreciate what you can about them. Reducing your expectations of others will make you much happier and allow you to accept the things you cannot change.

Don't do a favor for someone and then expect something in return. Remember, you are only concerned about pursuing excellence within yourself. Favors and good deeds are not a form of currency and should not be treated as such. Expecting someone to reciprocate a favor is setting yourself for disappointment. In the vast majority of cases, your goodwill will in fact be rewarded, but ever *expect* it.

Cutting People Off

You should only decide to eliminate a person from your life when they are causing you harm in some way. That can be physically, emotionally, socially, or simply that they are a chronic source of negative energy. You may find that your life is full of people who act impulsively, selfishly, or show little regard for those around them. These people may be benign entities. Once you have figured them out, you will know how to deal with them in terms of mitigating the impact of their bad behavior. There's no need to cut these types off completely — you may find that despite their character defects, you are still able to establish a connection of mutual respect. However, there are always a few cunning and manipulative people who actively work to degrade you. There are individuals who are extremely spiritually immature and live solely for their own egos. These individuals will oftentimes use others to boost their own self-worth at the total expense of their victims. These are the types of people that you must completely eliminate and avoid. Attempt to be at peace when you think of them, holding no animosity in your heart. Your mitigating action in dealing with these outliers is to completely eliminate any influence they would have on your life. Don't attempt retaliation! Simply acknowledge that person as they are and walk away.

Chapter 17: Learning to Cultivate and Cherish the Diamonds in our Lives

What is a diamond? Something so rare and precious that it has tremendous value. Undoubtedly you have a few people who are diamonds in your life. They are the people whom you can turn to when things are tough, who never talk behind your back, and who always have your best interest at heart. They are usually friends and family who have become permanent fixtures in our lives and unfortunately we often take them for granted. It's a strange phenomenon of human nature that we tend to pursue those people who seem distant, unavailable, and emotionally indifferent towards us. When we are immersed in our own egos, we feel that it's important that everyone likes us, invites us to things, and values our friendship. Once we know that a person is always in our corner, we tend to devalue the relationship, and often fail to cultivate a deeper connection with that person.

This does not always happen of course. Hopefully you have the understanding to value the diamonds in your life. The older you get, you come to realize that the only people who truly matter *are* the diamonds. There will always be socially malicious individuals, and there will always be people who attempt to use and abuse you. These people simply do not matter. As we've already discussed, identify and eliminate these people's influence from your life. Simultaneously, you should also identify those who support you the most and commit yourself to place extra attention on these folks. The relationships that you foster with the diamonds in your life are more valuable than anything you will ever own materially.

I won't tell you a story of a rich celebrity who died in their home without friends, only when it was too late realizing that the things they really valued in life could not be bought with money. I won't tell these stories although there are many because this book is about happiness and positivity. I want you to know however, that there is nothing on this Earth more precious than a true friend. Friendship is earned through acceptance and love for one another, and that has nothing to do with money.

Cherish your S.O. Above All

By far the brightest diamond in your life should be your significant other. This is the person with whom you share your life and dreams with. This relationship needs to be fostered above all others. Taking time to enjoy life with them, not through mindless time wasters such as TV or alcohol, but by actually engaging in conscious activities together (ACE), will bring you significantly closer. You'll develop a sense of appreciation for this person that you hadn't known previously.

There's no need to do an exercise to identify the diamonds in your life because you already know who they are. Usually there's 2-3 people in a person's life who fall into this category. Think of these people as the most precious thing in the world - and when you interact with them, you'll find that your approach is different. When you recognize the diamonds in your life as incredible gifts, you'll naturally want to care for them above all else.

It's easy to identify the diamonds in our lives because they are the people who make us feel at peace, recharged, and fully alive.

They care about us as equals and don't use us as leverage for their egos. I encourage my girlfriend to spend time with her childhood friends because I see the way she lights up after spending some time with them. After one weekend trip with her girlfriends, she told me how they all went out to a bar and laughed so hard all night that her stomach muscles were sore the next day. Her friends are the diamonds in her life that serve to renew, validate, and support her.

We oftentimes take for granted or take advantage of the diamonds in our lives — oftentimes unconsciously. It's an odd characteristic of human nature to want to seek out the approval of the worst people in our lives. This is our ego in action and the primary method in which narcissists trap others to support their enormous egos. When someone criticizes us, if we living in our egos, our first reaction is to be defensive, followed by a desire to prove to the person criticizing that you are worthwhile. In this case, you are putting your own self-value in the hands of the criticizer. In reality, that person has no business making value judgements against you, and their opinion of you is absolutely irrelevant. Breaking away from our ego-self is the key to dismissing those who would aim to control and manipulate by narcissistic means. We can easily accomplish this through a daily meditation practice.

As you start to live more mindfully and within your true self versus your ego-self, you will naturally gravitate towards less need for external validation. In other words, you'll be less clingy. This will enable you to take pity on those narcissists who require external validation, and to foster healthy relationships with our diamonds.

Maintaining diamond level relationships can take some work. However, you will find that the rewards are well worth the effort, and your relationships with these wonderful people will be solidified and strengthened. Here are some ways in which you can work to maintain your diamond-level relationships:

- **Make notes of birthdays and send a real life card.** Facebook notes won't work here. Take the time to write a note and drop it in the mail. Nowadays people are blown away by this simple act. Include a small gift if you like.

- **Actively seek to include them in your life.** Invite your diamonds to dinner parties, trips, and anything where you can spend quality time with them.

- **Be Loyal.** Never talk badly of your diamonds and discourage negative talk which involves this person. Be a constant cheerleader for them, even when they are not around.

- **Give them the benefit of the doubt.** Always assume that your diamonds have your best interest in mind. Assuming the best casts them in a special light, and will generate strong vibrational energy which serves to strengthen and validate the connection you have.

- **Celebrate their achievements.** This is huge - always be legitimately happy for their accomplishments in life. Celebrate with them. This is another simple test to determine if a person fits within the diamond category. If someone responds to your accomplishments with hate, jealousy, and/or trolls your social media page, they are likely living within their ego. Egos like to compare and contrast whereas true friendships revolve around sharing joy with each other.

- **Don't keep score.** I'm sure that you have a friend who is so close to you that, even if you didn't talk or see one another for 10 years, you could pick right back up from where you left off, without animosity or hurt over the absence. True friendship is timeless and there's no score being kept. Diamond-level friendships will naturally balance themselves out in terms of effort and support but neither party is really keeping score. Don't worry about the last time they contacted you or did you a favor - just continue to show them legitimate support.

EXERCISE 9

On a new piece of paper, write down all the diamonds in your life. There's no minimum or maximum number here. It's very possibly that your number is 0. If this is the case, don't worry - you will find one eventually. You may want to include this as one of your top manifestation goals if this is the case.

After you have listed each diamond in your life, next to their name make a note of how you plan to reconnect or strengthen your relationship with that person. For example, if you haven't spoken to your best friend in a while, you might write: "set up a weekly time to meet for coffee with Bob", as your action step.

CHAPTER 18: THE GIFT OF CRITICISM

"Criticism may not be agreeable, but it is necessary. It fulfils the same function as pain in the human body. It calls attention to an unhealthy state of things". - Winston Churchill

"The trouble with most of us is that we would rather be ruined by praise than saved by criticism." - Norman Vincent Peale

If we choose to talk negatively about other people, we need to be really careful not to throw those well-meaning individuals who may have criticized us in the past into the same category as those people whose goals are to demean and belittle as a method to boost their own egos. There are undoubtedly people in your life who have angered you through their criticism — criticism which you may have perceived as unjust. Usually when we have a strong reaction to criticism, it's because there is some element of truth in it. We become angry because we view truthful criticism as a direct threat to our egos.

Avoiding criticism is the safe route that leads to stagnation of character and mind. Humans are incredibly complex social creatures and we rely on the positive and negative social feedback of others to improve ourselves. There is no power in isolation or avoidance. This isn't to say that we should shirk our alone time.

It's important to take time alone to meditate, pray, and recuperate our energies. When we face criticism head on, it can be painful because it forces us to open up our hearts and drop our ego-defence mechanisms. Because of this, we should take the following 3-step approach to facing criticism head on:

- **Retreat** - listen to the criticism. Make note of it for future analysis.

- **Regroup** - determine whether the criticism was valid or simply ego-boosting behavior.

- **Re-engage** - if criticism was valid, engage with a new action plan for change, otherwise ignore and approach the person with love and acceptance, knowing that they are prone to ego-boosting behavior. In extreme cases you may choose to eliminate them from your life if their chronic, ego-boosting criticism begins to inhibit your safety, livelihood, or overall sense of peace.

If You're Mad, That's Your Ego

Becoming angry at criticism is an egocentric behavior. When we are able to externally observe the criticism, we detach our self-worth from the person's words. Only with this detachment are we able to successfully determine whether or not the criticism is valid. During the regrouping stage, we take the time to be alone and analyze the criticism, free from emotions. Look at it externally.

If you find that the criticism was simply intended to reduce your own ego and support the ego of another, then your best course of action is to ignore it. Ignoring egocentric criticism takes all the power out of the other person's words. You can even laugh to yourself when they attempt to boost their ego because you have identified the cause of their behavior. Lashing out, or responding with insults is oftentimes temporarily effective but is ultimately a form of ego war that leaves everyone depleted.

Protect Yourself First

It is vitally important to learn to protect yourself from those who are strongly ego driven. Individuals who are strongly ego driven have not matured enough spiritually to understand their true inherent worth as eternal beings. This isn't their fault — they are on a different path than you in terms of spiritual maturity. They are still living inside their ego, and external people and objects are providing them with a sense of self-worth. Egos love to feel better than others. An ego loves to point out differences and perceived deficiencies even when there aren't any. Egos are very delicate things and require lots of external validation to stay alive.

You are not responsible for anyone's spiritual maturity other than your own. If you find that you are often criticized by someone who is attempting to support their ego, you should view this person as you would a child. When children say or do something that is immature, we understand and have some degree of empathy because we know that it is partially beyond their control due to the fact that they are still learning about the world. Egocentric people are still developing. They are like spiritual children. Hence we approach them with empathy and compassion.

Egocentric people can be very dangerous in extreme cases. When you combine spiritual immaturity with a high level of intelligence it oftentimes results in a person who is extremely clever in their dealings with others. Their ego boosting behavior may not be as overt. More often than not, they will criticize or attempt to belittle you in more subtle ways. You must identify and protect yourself from this type of person. In most cases, the best practice will be to limit their influence in your life as much as possible. If possible, completely eliminate them from your life. If, at a later time, they have developed a greater level of spiritual maturity, you may reengage with them.

Be Thankful for Criticism

If we find that the criticism is valid, be thankful. Criticism is a wonderful opportunity to improve. Everyone makes mistakes. Everyone performs at a suboptimal level at times. However, only the spiritually mature individual can accept their own errors. Acceptance of imperfection is a hallmark of spiritual maturity as a human being. If you find that the criticism is true, make the necessary changes to correct course. Do not hold animosity towards the criticizer. View this person outside of the criticism and be thankful for the special gift they have given you. A true enemy will not criticize you. A real enemy allows you to continue to fail and fall short. If you find a person who offers you legitimate and real criticism, do not eliminate that person from your life. Although it may hurt, their criticism can serve to make you dramatically stronger.

Keep it Private

Once you have decided to take action to correct a behavior that has come to your attention through the gift of criticism, do not tell the criticizer or anyone else about your plans to change. Just do it. Put together an action plan and do it. Telling others your goals is pointless and can alert the truly malicious people in your life to sidetrack your attempts at improvement. Stay on path, have faith that you will succeed in reaching your goal or altering your behavior, and the world and people will change around you as you change yourself. Making fundamental changes in our own lives is no one's business but our own so keep it private.

EXERCISE 10

Take out a piece of paper and draw four columns. In column 1, list out the top twelve people of significance in your life. These will be people such as your significant other, your boss, or your best friend. In column two, answer the yes or no question: *"Is this person a positive influence in my life?"* In column three, answer another yes or no question, *"Is there a chance that my perception is inaccurate?"* To answer this question accurately, you will need to spend some time thinking about the person. You may even need to seek the counsel of trusted friends to ensure that your perception is truly accurate. Seeking the external perceptions of others can be a good source of data by which to adjust your perception barometer. After you've done some critical and objective thinking about this person, only then will you be able to accurately determine if they are truly a negative or positive influence in your life. If you find that you answer "no" to column two and three for a person, you should take immediate action to limit that person's role in your life. In this case, use column four to write out how you plan to remove this person from your life quickly. If however, you answer "yes" to column three, use column four to rewrite a new and positive perception of that person. This will serve as a new transforming belief about that person. In most cases, you will find that your relationship with that individual changes almost instantly. People will respond to your positive thought energy about them. People like people who like and respect them. Positive energy and affectation can be sensed, and the other person's brain will be more receptive to your presence. Just like you, their brain is working to protect itself from threats. Eliminating your negative energy through transforming your beliefs about them will immediately open their mind to your energy. Through this powerful method, you can transform enemies into friends and negative people into positive influences in your life. It's important to understand here that you are not controlling the person's thoughts since that is impossible. What you are doing is controlling your own perception of that person and in turn, their perception of you will change. Our perceptions, when aligned with our beliefs, will always result in manifestation as the universe seeks congruence between your thought energy and the external reality of your world.

EXERCISE 11

From the above exercise, take the ten positive transformative beliefs that you wrote down in column three and write them on your index cards. Place this stack of index cards next to your bathroom mirror. Each morning after completing your gratitude exercises, pick up your index cards and while looking in the mirror, say each one aloud several times. Doing this will reinforce these transforming beliefs. As we discussed earlier, beliefs are long held and have a powerful hold on your mental condition. You have the power to change them, but it's important to continually reinforce and strengthen your new way of thinking to prevent reversion to the negative thought energy.

CHAPTER 19: SHOW ME THE LOVE!

"Who is rich? He that enjoys his portion". - Ben Franklin

"Abundance is not something we acquire. It is something we tune into". - Dr. Wayne Dyer

Your biggest goal in the receiving stage is to truly *feel* what it's like to have your desire. Before the object of your desire actually manifests into your life you must have already entered a mindset where you are consciously and actively feeling what that is like. For example, if you desire to own your dream car, go to the dealership and sit in it. Test drive it. Imagine deeply that you own it now. Take pictures with it - videos of yourself with the car. Anything that will serve to trigger the emotional responses associated with having it *now*.

Once you become accustomed to experiencing the emotions that your object of desire brings, the manifestation will seem only natural. When the object or person shows up in your life, instead of being a pleasant surprise, it will be a pleasant confirmation of your current feelings.

If you are doing a good job of successfully generating the feelings of having your object of desire in the present moment yet you are not seeing the object or person manifest, just stay calm. Trust that the universe is putting into motion the steps and situations necessary to create a congruence between your emotional state and your physical state. In other words, have faith it's on its way!

Having faith that the universe will deliver is crucial. As part of this faith, never test the universe or look for physical signs of manifestation. Traditional scientific methods of observation and experimentation don't work well when attempting to understand the Law of Attraction. Instead, you need to rely more on your feelings and beliefs over reason. Reason has its place and we can't live functionally without it. However, when we are concerned with manifesting things into our lives, we need to sometimes focus on things that are subjective, irrational, and obscure. Mainly we are dealing with our emotions.

Emotions are powerful sources of vibrational energy — both good and bad. When we can control our minds to generate feelings of a positive nature, we can harness the vibrational energy we create to manifest anything we desire. Once you master this ability, it becomes apparent very quickly how much power and control we truly have over our personal reality.

Why is it bad when we test the universe or look for signs that the Law of Attraction is working? Why is it bad when we look for outward signs of manifestation? It's simple — when we do this, we are sending negative vibrational energy that states, *"I don't trust that my desire will manifest and therefore I am seeking an external sign rather than trusting the universe to deliver."* The universe is highly attuned to your mind and the vibrational energy it generates. If you are constantly testing and seeking outward validation, you are basically telling the universe that you don't believe that the Law of Attraction will hold true. Unfortunately, the universe hears your message and delivers as promised. The universe delivers every time, no matter what you are thinking!

Gratitude

"Be thankful for what you have; you'll end up having more. If you concentrate on what you don't have, you will never, ever have enough".
– *Oprah Winfrey*

"Gratitude unlocks the fullness of life. It turns what we have into enough, and more. It turns denial into acceptance, chaos to order, confusion to clarity. It can turn a meal into a feast, a house into a home, a stranger into a friend". – *Melody Beattie*

Gratitude is vitally important in the receiving stage. Once you receive the object or person of your desire, you should give thanks daily, preferably morning and night. Thanking the universe solidifies your gains, and generates even more positive feelings of having it now. Since like attracts like, these positive feelings will generate even more positive feelings which will result in even greater physical manifestations in your life. Always give abundant thanks to what the universe has brought into your life! Be thankful for family, friends, pets, jobs, money, etc. There is nothing too small to say thank you for!

Putting yourself into a state of gratitude is so vitally important to every stage of the creation process that an entire book could be written about it. As you *ask*, *believe*, and *receive*, it's important to focus on gratitude throughout. Gratitude is the glue that locks the interactions together and allows the magic to happen. The moment that you start to take things for granted is the moment that the Law of Attraction falls apart. If you've manifested things and people into your life, be grateful and stay grateful! If not, those things and people will not be around for long. You can bring whatever you desire into your life, and keep it that way forever - as long as you continue to live in a constant state of gratitude.

EXERCISE 12

Take out the list you created from exercise four. This is the list where you wrote down everything that you want to manifest into your life. Focus on the top ten things for now.

Use a new sheet of paper for each desire listed. At the top of each separate sheet of paper, write out the desire at the top. For example, you might write, *"New Bentley SUV"* at the top of one.

Under that, we are going to create a manifestation plan for each desire.

Let's start with gratitude. Start by writing out the following: *"I am so happy and grateful now that I have X in my life!"*

Next under that, list any directed action steps that you can immediately think of that could put you closer to this goal. Be as quick and as loose as possible and don't avoid entertaining any and all possibilities that could aid you in realizing this goal. Note that inspired action, the most powerful type of action, cannot be written down since it only presents itself in the moment the universe chooses. Instead of writing down inspired actions, simply write out the following statement:

"I choose to be open and receptive to any and all signs that the universe sends to me. I know that X is on its way!"

Lastly, briefly describe your life when your desire comes into your life. Use feeling verbs, and describe in as great a detail as possible how it feels right now to have the object of your desire. For example, if you are wishing for a new car, describe how it feels to drive to work, pick up your friends, etc. Describe the sound of the stereo, the feel of the road, and the way the leather seats feel. The more feelings you can generate in your writing the better.

This exercise is meant to bring together the entire manifestation process of *believe*, *act*, and *receive* on a single sheet of paper. It will help you immensely to put your mind in a positive and receptive state. The goal here is to generate the feelings of having it now, while being grateful that it is already on its way. Throughout this process, practice faith that your desire will come into your life. Anytime you sense a positive emotion while you write, stop to allow yourself to fully embrace and amplify that emotion as much as possible.

Chapter 20: Maintain and Adjust

"Life is the continuous adjustment of internal relations to external relations". - Herbert Spencer

"Successful people maintain a positive focus in life no matter what is going on around them. They stay focused on their past successes rather than their past failures, and on the next action steps they need to take to get them closer to the fulfilment of their goals rather than all the other distractions that life presents to them". - Jack Canfield

If you think the raucous political antics of the 2016 American presidential race are setting records for party infighting and extremism, take a look back in history to the year 1912 when Theodore Roosevelt was running against Woodrow Wilson. As a two-time Republican president, Roosevelt should have handed the reins of power over to his successor. However, Roosevelt wanted to run again for the presidency, despite the opinions of the majority of his Republican colleagues. In a complete act of rogue political determinism, Roosevelt switched from the Republican Party to the Progressive Party. He set about the country determined to win a third term as president. Despite what the rules were, and despite what the majority of people believed about the political process, Theodore Roosevelt created his own path to reach his goal. Roosevelt didn't accept the rules that limited him, so he rewrote the rules of the game.

On October 14, 1912, Theodore Roosevelt stood in front of a Milwaukee hotel and address a large crowd. Just moments earlier, he had been shot nearly point blank range in the chest by an unemployed saloon keeper. The man had been taken away by police, and despite the wishes of Roosevelt's staff, he refused to go to the hospital. The miracle that Roosevelt was alive was due to the fact that he was wearing a thick overcoat, and inside of his breast pocket he was carrying his 50 page speech along with a sturdy metal case for his eyeglasses. The bullet penetrated his coat, the speech, and the eyeglass case before lodging an inch into his chest. Rather than call off the speech, Roosevelt used it to his advantage. He opened his speech by stating, "Friends, I ask you to be as quiet as possible. I don't know if you fully understand that I have just been shot."

He then proceeded to open his coat and reveal his blood stained shirt to the crowd. Everyone in attendance was in awe of this man and felt that whatever he had to say must be of incredible importance. Roosevelt went on to give his 90 minute speech, enchanting the crowd and winning their support. He finally left for the hospital amid cheers and shouts of support. Theodore Roosevelt was so focused on the outcome that he refused to allow being shot to derail the vision he had for himself. He immediately shifted course to adapt to the new challenge, and used the hardship to his best advantage.

Once we see our desires manifested in our lives, sometimes we find that what we wished for really wasn't what we wanted. For example, if you manifested the girl or guy of your dreams into your life, only to find that they are inclined to cheat, you most likely did not offer a detailed enough request to the universe. Your thought energy needs to be very specific. The universe does not care about your intent, it merely responds to your request. If your request is vague, the universe will offer the fastest solution, which may not always be in-line with what you intended. The universe is only concerned with reaching a state of congruence between external reality and the thought reality of your mind. It seeks the quickest and most effective path for that to happen.

Additionally, once we reach our goals or achieve our object of desire, we may start to get lazy with our positive thought generation. When this happens, usually we tend to fall back on our long-held beliefs. If these long term beliefs are negative or limiting, then we can see the degradation or even the elimination of our manifestations. To prevent this, we need to enter a maintenance phase in the manifestation process. A very simple way to do this is simply to establish the habit of thanking the universe every morning for the good things in your life. This generates feelings of gratitude. Gratitude is incredibly powerful because it taps into pure positive emotion. Since like attracts like, showing gratitude will solidify your gains and bring even more of the good stuff into your life.

Beyond practicing gratitude on a daily basis, it's important to engage in behaviours and activities that will bring joy to your life. Instead of watching a depressing documentary, choose to watch a goofy comedy that makes you laugh. Anything that generates laughter is powerful medicine which actively alters your vibrational thought energy. Use laughter and comedy as a tool in the manifestation process.

Choose to spend your time only with those people who validate and encourage you. It may be impossible to eliminate all the energy suckers from your life, but limiting their effectiveness is easy to do. When someone insults or manipulates us, it hurts because it is a direct assault to our ego, which is tied to our identity and hence our sense of self-worth. The easiest and most effective technique for developing a bullet-proof personality is to establish a consistent habit of meditating daily.

Meditation Makes a Strong Mind

Meditation is like going to the gym for your mind. When we meditate, we consciously and non-judgementally observe our own thoughts and beliefs. Observing a negative thought and acknowledging it as something outside of ourselves takes a lot of the pressure off. If a thought is external to our being, that means that it has no bearing on our identity. We quickly learn that negative people and situations do not contribute to our sense of self. We are eternal beings.

Oftentimes the brain is engaged in future simulation or even worse, agonising over the past. The place where we find our most happiness is in the *present*. In the present moment, we find no fear, shame, guilt, or regret. What we find instead, is pure joy. In the now, we fully appreciate the beauty around us. In the now, we approach existence completely non-judgementally. In the now, we also find our most gratitude,

Training your mind to stop projecting into the future or dwelling on the past is called mindfulness. Being mindful helps you to see how most things in life really aren't that important. It "turns the volume down" on drama and brings a wonderful sense of calm. Through mindfulness, we can also focus our thought energy to generate very powerful images and feelings which will serve to accelerate the manifestation process.

How then, can you start to become more mindful in your day to day life? Start by finding a quiet room in our house where you can sit for up to thirty minutes undisturbed. Sit on the floor, cross-legged and with your back straight. Close your eyes and begin to focus on your breathing. Breathe in through your nose and ex-hale through your mouth. Take at least 2 seconds to inhale and 2 full seconds to exhale. Focus on nothing else but your breath-ing. At first, you will sense your mind fighting back against the lack of sensory inputs. The egoic mind loves to have a cornu-copia of varied sense input with which to cling to. The purpose of the egoic mind is to shape your identity around the existence of external objects. The sense that things are attached to your self-worth is completely illusory in nature. When we meditate, we discover our true selves — the inner being that nothing or no one can touch.

Elimination of the egoic mind is not the goal. We simply wish to gain more control and awareness over it. This means that we are no longer slaves to our emotions or desires. We can detach and examine things objectively without connecting it to a sense of self. You may find that once you start practicing meditation on a daily basis, your goals for manifesting things into your life begin to change. Having a new found and solid sense of self along with an inner peace, you will intuitively gravitate toward those things that bring you joy without dependence. Dependence on objects or people come straight from the ego. We do need the ego to function however, since egoic desires are what drive us to accomplish almost everything. If you want a new car, want it because you love it — not because you feel it will complete you as a person or make you seem more worthwhile in the eyes of others.

Exercise 13

Upon waking in the morning, take some personal time to give thanks for good things in your life. A good place to do this is in the shower. Saying "thank you" aloud is very powerful. Try saying aloud *thank you for bringing x into my life*. You will find that this dramatically changes your mental state in the morning. You will start the day mentally and spiritually energized, excited for the possibilities ahead. This is an easy habit to establish and pays dividends immediately. Make sure to list all the positive things in your life no matter how small. The universe takes joy in your joy, and will respond to your positive acknowledgements.

As discussed in the previous chapter which examined religious transformation as a model we can use to tap into the power of faith, establishing routines to maintain our beliefs is vitally important. To recap what was suggested as possible routines:

- Give thanks every morning (Daily)

- Read a list of Affirmations ex: "I am so grateful and joyous now that..." (Weekly)

- Read books on Positive thinking and the Law of Attraction (Bi-Weekly)

- Visit Law of Attraction websites and blogs (Daily)

- Watch uplifting programs and comedies on TV

- Meditate for 20 minutes (1-2 times Daily)

Affirmations

Affirmations can be a great tool to help us maintain our beliefs. They combat the mind's tendency to fall back on long held beliefs. As long as those beliefs are positive and help us achieve our goals, we have nothing to worry about. However, most people suffer from some form of habitual negative thoughts stemming from long held negative beliefs. We've talked a lot about transforming those negative beliefs into positive ones. The reality is that your mind is like a record playing on a record player. Long term beliefs are like the grooves in the album, and the needle on the record player doesn't want to change course. In order to solidify the newly held positive beliefs, you must take measures to reinforce those beliefs on a continual basis. One very effective method of doing this is through the use of positive affirmations.

What are affirmations? They are simply positive statements which we write down and refer to often. They describe a desired situation or goal. We want to repeat this preferably daily in order to reprogram the mind with the new belief pattern.

Your Self-Talk Programs your Mind

You may not realize it, but most likely you already are using affirmations of the negative sort. The majority of people hold some long held beliefs about themselves or others and those beliefs are reflected in their constant self-talk. For example, if a person holds the view that they are fundamentally not worthy of being loved, they may downplay the significance of the words *"I love you"* when told by family or friends. There are many examples of negative self-talk that have a negative impact on our state of mind. Meditation is once again the best tool to be able to tune in to your thoughts and become aware of your inner dialogue. Those who have never been exposed to mindfulness may find it difficult to slow their thoughts down long enough to identify their own self-talk. Through meditation, we learn to control the mind and become aware of our inner dialogue.

Think of affirmations as the programming language by which you can reprogram the computer which is your mind. When we use affirmations on a regular basis, we are creating powerful, repetitive instructions that serve to reiterate positively held beliefs. We can create affirmations for anything that we wish to achieve or simply to reinforce a newly held belief. I have often used affirmations in sports to build confidence. I once used affirmations along with feelings of having it now to score a goal in a soccer game. My dad was coming to watch me play, the first game he had ever attended since I started playing soccer as an adult. I wanted badly to score a goal while he was there. The days leading up to the game, I said aloud to myself while driving, showering, or anytime I was alone, the following affirmation: *"I consistently score goals"* and *"Scoring goals comes easily and naturally to me"*. I paired that with feeling generation and stated my request to the universe in the form of *"I am so happy and ecstatic that I scored a goal in front of my dad!*". I allowed myself to visualize the discussion with him after the game — I imagined each detail of him patting me on the back and congratulating me on my goal. Do you know what happened? Well, I did score a goal in the first half of that game - it was a long shot from near mid pitch (we were playing indoor soccer), and the ball curved down from high right arcing down over the goalie's head just out of his reach. Everyone was blown away by the goal because it did look spectacular since it was such a long shot. I saw my dad up in the stands jump from his seat and pump his fist in the air. I experienced the exact same emotions that I did during my visualization exercises at that time. During half time, I continued to use the affirmation, *"I consistently score goals."* I played the second half with several missed shots on goal. With less than five minutes left in the game, me and a team-mate had a break away that resulted in a two on one situation with the keeper. As we approached the goal, my teammate shot a quick pass to me. Instinctually I received the ball hard on the instep of my foot, and it reflected directly into the lower corner of the goal. I walked away from that game having scored two goals which rarely had occurred in the past. My dad was really impressed and we had fun socializing with the team afterwards. My use of affirmations, a faith based request to universe, visual-ization exercises, and generating the feelings of having it now, all worked together to quickly manifest my desire to score not one but two goals in front of my dad.

A Self-Talk Resource

One of the best books I've ever read concerning affirmations is The Self-Talk Solution by Shad Helmstetter. It contains over 2,500 personal affirmations organized into useful categories cov-ering everything from health to interpersonal communication. I used this book in my late teens when I joined the Army to over-come low self-esteem, shyness, and various other insecurities. I can say that the affirmations in this book started me on the jour-ney to radically transform myself for the better. Today, I still use affirmations, but in conjunction with the Law of Attraction to see rapid manifestation.

Patience is Key

While there are desires that can manifest instantly and it's true that time means nothing to the universe, there are situations that may take some time to manifest in your life. The universe will respond in kind to the vibrations that you are generating, whether they be negative or positive. We know from previous chapters that when we learn to generate the feelings of having it now, we are creating powerful vibrations and sending those out to the universe. If reality hasn't yet caught up to those powerful vibrations, **the universe will do everything within its power to correct the disparity between your thoughts and what is currently manifested in your reality.**

Let's say that I want to manifest one billion dollars. That is a lot of money by anyone's standard. There's no lottery or casino on Earth with that much money in its prize pool. It will likely take some time for all the elements to fall into place in order for your desire to be able to manifest. You may need to start a business, invest profits, and catch some desirable breaks in the business world in order to achieve your goal of one billion dollars. There are no limitations to the law of attraction although time for a goal to manifest will vary depending on the complexity of your request. For some goals to manifest, you will need to be patient.

Patience means that you never question whether or not the desired outcome will come — it will! Patience means that you continue to apply directed and inspired action and constantly practice faith. Applying belief and using visualization techniques, as well as applying Law of Attraction amplifiers such as optimum health, affirmations, a supportive group of people, and a tidy and well organized environment will help to speed up your desired goal. However, big goals sometimes require some time. That's not to say that time is a limiting factor in every situation. Some goals, no matter how big, can be manifested in a day. Sometimes that goal may take years to arrive. The key here is to understand one fundamental truth: It's on its way!

Chapter 21: LOA Amplifier: Your Optimum Health

"You're in pretty good shape for the shape you are in". –Dr. Suess

"To keep the body in good health is a duty... otherwise we shall not be able to keep our mind strong and clear". – The Buddha

The body is intrinsically linked to the mind. When we practice mindfulness, we learn through meditation that we exist as infinite beings external of our egos and the delicate strategies that it employs to make us feel special and better than others. Our sense of self is truly external to our bodies, however, there is a physical link between mind and body that is inescapable. In philosophy, the idea that the soul exists externally from the body is called dualism. The idea that the mind and body are one is called monism.

Traditional Western religion and philosophy teaches that the body is a vessel in which the soul resides (dualism). The idea is that when our bodies die, our souls still exist and then move into another form of existence outside the confines of our physical world. For Christians, this would be called heaven.

The idea that the soul and body are two separate things is wildly appealing to our egos. Our egos want to live forever. Egos want to maintain their carefully constructed sense of worth and that means sustaining the status quo. Viewing the body and mind as one is a less ego-centric and more accurate way to view what philosophers refer to as the 'mind-body problem'.

The Buddha taught that the mind and the body are distinct yet dependent. Although our true selves are external and infinite in nature, the expression of our true self is fundamentally dependent upon our physical state. Sounds kinda tricky? Let me offer an analogy. When you wake up in the morning, you probably would not describe yourself as being "fully conscious". In fact, you might even require a few cups of coffee before you even attempt to engage with the world. In this period of time while you are waking up, you can clearly see how the condition of your mind is intrinsically linked to your your physical state. The quality of our conscious experience is directly tied to to the quality of our physical being.

Solving the mind-body problem isn't our goal in this book. You are free to come to your own conclusions regarding the existence of a soul. You may choose to believe that your thoughts, perceptions, and sense of self are simply the result of very complex physical processes which occur in the brain. On the other end of the spectrum, you may choose to believe a more traditional dualistic view. What is important here is that you understand that no matter what philosophic views you hold in regard to this problem, the mind and the body are bound and dependent upon one another. We can't argue that our physical bodies aren't temporary. We will all die one day. What happens after death is not important at this time. What is important, is understanding that our mind and bodies exist in an interdependent partnership.

If we accept this notion, then we look at health in a more sacred manner. How important exercise, eating right, and abstaining from harmful substances becomes when we view it as interdependent to our soul! Clean living and improving our health should be done with a holistic approach, understanding that by improving the quality of our health, we can fully engage our conscious energy. Because our consciousness is bound by our physical state, we can only fully connect with ourselves and others when we are functionally fit and healthy. Whenever we are sick, tired, sleepy, drunk, or intoxicated with drugs, we are severely limiting our ability to experience high quality relationships with others. Also when we are in these physically limited states, we suppress our ability to engage fully with the wonders of our world, as well as with ourselves. When we are physically debilitated in some way, we are less conscious. When we are less conscious, we are not generating very strong vibrational energy with our thoughts. When we are physically healthy and strong, we are mentally fully engaged with the world and thus we have the ability to generate extremely powerful thought vibrations. The universe will respond much faster and with more intensity to the thoughts generated from an optimally fit mind.

Another way to think of the brain is as a highly complex, highly tuned system from which arises the mind while being extremely sensitive to vibrational energy around it. Your brain can be used as a tool to collect and generate vibrational energy. With a highly fit brain, we can generate intensely powerful thought vibrations.

Your goal should be optimum health. This doesn't necessarily mean that you have to have a six pack or under 10% body fat. Most people work out and exercise with hedonistic goals in mind. In other words, they are more concerned with looking good as a method of boosting their own egos. Approach healthy living and exercise as a spiritual pursuit and you will see amazing results in your ability to create your own reality though the Law of Attraction. As your body becomes stronger, your mind will follow. As your mind becomes stronger and more alert, you will find it easier and easier to generate the positive feelings and thoughts necessary to manifest your goals.

What are some ways that we can become physically healthier? Why do I choose to include a section on physical health in a book about the Law of Attraction? Simply put, being in shape will make it much easier to manifest your desires. Improving your health should be approached as a lifestyle, not just a series of intermittent actions. In other words, you need to establish healthy, daily habits that will serve to keep you in optimum condition.

Some key areas to consider when improving your health:

- Cardiovascular health

- Strength training

- Nutrition

- Time in Nature

- Sleep quality

- Laughter

- Relaxation

- Moderation (with substances)

- Sexual health

These are not listed in order of importance. They are all important to overall optimum health. Always consult your doctor prior to making radical lifestyle adjustments. You want to start by making sure you have the green light to start exercising. Use whatever resources you can find to motivate, guide, and inspire you towards your fitness goals. Join a gym, join a recreational football team, etc. Fitness is an ongoing and constant pursuit and takes many forms. Have fun with it and don't allow the pursuit to become a stressor itself. It takes guts and determination to become optimally fit, but the outcome is well worth the effort! Not only will you live longer, be happier, and engage more fully with the world, but you will find that your ability to manifest things into your life using the Law of Attraction will be significantly enhanced!

Nowadays, I spend a lot of time in the Alps skiing and hiking with friends. Where I live in the Rhineland-Pflaz region of Germany, we have some of the best mountain bike trails in Europe, and I am constantly out on a long ride with my dog in tow. I love to climb too, and usually spend a few days a week climbing or bouldering in the local area. Although I'm in my forties, I still skateboard and will drop in at the local skate park from time to time. I run a few half-marathons every year with friends, and I love running through the woods near my home. I also train in jujitsu once or twice a week. Being active has become such an intrinsic part of my life that I cannot fathom the idea of being a couch potato. If I'm lying on the couch and watching a documentary or movie, it's with a sense that I earned my lazy time. It feels great to chill out with sore legs, an athletic heart, and a calm mind.

CHAPTER 22: LOA AMPLIFIER: YOUR IMMEDIATE ENVIRONMENT

"The connection between health and the dwelling of the population is one of the most important that exists." — *Florence Nightingale*

When a person is consistently emitting positive vibrational thought energy, one of the things we see is an immediate reflection in their environment. A person in a positive frame, with high self-awareness and high self-esteem, will naturally gravitate towards a neat and orderly house, car, and office space. Disorganization and clutter are the direct results of negative thought patterns.

If cleaning and organization aren't coming naturally and easily to you, this is a clear indication that you have some internal work to do. Don't be discouraged however, because we can jumpstart the process and move toward a positive frame just by taking the time to do a thorough house cleaning.

Just as with any concept, it helps immensely to understand exactly *why* this works the way it does.

Think of the times in your life when you have felt truly organized and your home and office have felt super clean. It feels great doesn't it? When you come home at the end of the day and you open the door to your house, and everything is in its place, and the house smells fresh and clean, it immediately puts you into a positive and organized mental state. Of course, a messy house will do just the opposite.

The effects of your immediate environment is something that is often overlooked by practitioners of the Law of Attraction. As we've learned in previous chapters, the Law of Attraction is something that we have observed to be true in every situation, every time. The Law of Attraction is mysterious in that it doesn't follow exactly the normal laws of empirical science that we've come to expect. Just as Einstein described the strange world of quantum physics as "spooky action at a distance", so too are elements of the Law of Attraction that we just can't explain with traditional scientific reasoning. We do know however, that it for sure works and we can identify amplifiers that help it to work better and faster.

Clutter Affects Your Mind

Think of your mind as an extremely sensitive instrument. Day in and day out, the things that we expose our mind to will start to affect our subconscious in ways that we may not be aware of. A messy and disorganized house is the same as a physical and visual negative affirmation that says *"you are not worth a clean space"*, and *"your life is not under control"*. These are powerful and subtle negative physical reminders that will serve to consistently move you toward a negative state. Even though you may be doing everything else right — showing gratitude, acting directed and inspired, visualizations, positive verbal affirmations, meditation, and exercise — if you have a messy home, it will work against all the positive things you are doing and will hamper your ability to manifest. It's like trying to swim with a lead weight tied around one of your feet! In order to swim, you must work extra hard just to stay afloat. Don't allow your personal space to drag you down. Keep your house, car, and office clean and organized and watch it serve as a multiplier to your manifestation efforts.

Feng Shui Works

The objects and space in your home reflect their own negative or positive energy back to you on a continual basis. This is why it's so important that you create a positive, uplifting, and refreshing space which will serve to bolster and support your positive mental frame. The idea of objects and space holding their own energy and directly interacting with your mind is not a new one. In the Chinese art of Feng Shui, this object-energy is known as qi. In Korea and Japan, it's been called gi and chi respectively for around 5,000 years. The Hindus call it Prana. The ancient Greeks know it as pneuma. The Buddhists call it Iung. The ancient Jews referred to this object-energy as ruah. Today, in Western philosophical thought, we refer to it as an element of the Law of Attraction. When something is so widely known and understood across cultures, it provides massive credibility to its existence, even though we can't prove it through standard scientific approaches.

In Feng Shui, there are some critical truths. Mainly, we should be aware that our physical environment plays a significant role in our overall health and mental well-being and that we have direct control over this.

In a recent study conducted by the Indiana University department of Physical Activity, researchers tracked the health and mental status of 998 African Americans between the ages of 49 and 65. They compared their levels of physical activity with the cleanliness of their homes. They found that those with the cleanest homes had the highest levels of health and life satisfaction. The researchers stated this was an unexpected finding as the causation was unknown. The correlation however, cannot be ignored.

Even more significant, is the study conducted by the Princeton University Neuroscience Institute - published in the Jan 2011 issue of The Journal of Neuroscience which focused expressly on the negative mental outcomes resulting from messy and unorganized living spaces. In their report, "Interactions of Top-Down and Bottom-Up Mechanisms in Human Visual Cortex", they state the following:

"Multiple stimuli present in the visual field at the same time compete for neural representation by mutually suppressing their evoked activity throughout visual cortex, providing a neural correlate for the limited processing capacity of the visual system".

In other words, if your house is a mess, your brain is immediately moved to an unfocused, disorganized state where information processing is limited. Over time, the presence of clutter and mess can wreak havoc on your mental acuity and ability to soundly reason. Cleaning your house and organizing your space restores the brain's ability to focus.

The above mentioned study was completed within the framework of traditional science using the scientific method. We can extrapolate from the results and conclude that since our brains are delicate instruments, and that because we know that the Law of Attraction is always working, clutter and mess will consistently affect us in negative ways. We can confidently reason that our ability to manifest will be severely limited in a messy house.

When I was in the US Army about twenty-five years ago, I experienced first-hand the power that a clean environment can bring about to one's mental state. I joined the Army at the age of seventeen with permission from my dad. I grew up in a household where my mom always did the laundry. I had never used a washing machine until I was shipped off to Army boot camp. During basic training, we lived a very regimented and controlled life and we had set times to do our laundry at night. I managed to get thorough boot camp ok but once I was sent off to my active duty location, I had some problems. Since I had never established a habit of doing laundry, I would often let my dirty clothes just pile up to the point where, having no more clean clothes, I was forced to wash a few shirts and underwear. I often found myself scrambling to wash clothes the night before work, and I almost constantly had a pile of dirty clothes on the floor in my barracks room. One day, we had a surprise inspection in the barracks. I could hear the sergeants yelling down the hall for everyone to step into the hall so I quickly moved my mountain of dirty clothes into my wall locker and barely was able to shut it closed. That day, the sergeant major was personally walking through to inspect the rooms. If you don't know, Sergeant Major is a God-like rank in the Army — the highest enlisted rank. When the sergeant major got to my room, he came in, checked my bed (which was made thankfully), checked the small refrigerator, yelled at me for having too much garbage in my trashcan, and turned to walk out. At the last minute, he eyed my wall locker and decided to open it up and look inside. The mountain of dirty clothes that I had stuffed in there spilled out onto the floor and actually covered his boots. Needless to say, he wasn't happy. As punishment, I was given sixty days of room inspections every morning. My first line supervisor was tasked with inspecting my room every morning to make sure I was doing my laundry and keeping everything clean and organized. Of course my immediate supervisor was pissed that he had to wake up early and come to my room every morning to inspect it. He made it really difficult on me and came in with an actual white glove every morning. For sixty days I lived in a semi-sterile environment. At first, it was tough because I was forced to form new habits, however, after a few weeks I found that I was feeling extremely confident and alert. Oddly, I felt more confident than I had ever felt in my life and I experienced a sense of well-being that I had not known previously. Coming home to my barracks room each night, knowing where each item I owned belonged, and always having things in perfect order, really freed my mind up in a very positive way. I didn't know it at the time, but the Law of Attraction was working in me. My super clean environment was constantly creating powerful visual affirmations that boosted my self-esteem, confidence, and ability to think clearly. On the fiftieth day of inspections, there was another surprise inspection for the entire barracks. The sergeant major was also present for this one. When he saw my room, he was shocked. The floor was so shiny that he could see himself in it. Later that day, he came over to our unit and had me come up to the front of the formation and presented me with a military coin. He "pardoned" the remaining ten days of inspections, and said that he had never seen a barracks room as clean as mine. From that experience, I learned how to clean as well as the importance of my physical environment to my overall happiness and mental clarity. To this day, I still strive to maintain a clean and organised space — not because I fear a surprise white glove inspection, but because I know that it will serve as a powerful multiplier to my manifestation efforts, as well as my general sense of peace and abundance.

Start with Your Kitchen

Want an immediate boost? Start with your kitchen. Wash the dishes, clean out the fridge, and wipe down all the surfaces. Take a break and then move to the next room. Go room by room until your entire house is in order. Then move on to your car and garage. If you're having trouble getting started, I highly recommend a book that I have come to love: The Life-Changing Magic of Tidying Up by Marie Kondo. In this amazing book, she talks about only keeping objects that "spark joy". If an object doesn't spark joy in you, you should throw it out. It's a very effective system for keeping your spaces clean and organized. Change your space and you'll start to see your reality change in response!

Chapter 23: LOA Amplifier: Your Positive Support Group

You've heard it said that no man is an island. That statement is true in so many ways. Self-help books and mindfulness training constantly preach that we can only be happy when we are happy with ourselves, limit the ego, and learn to live in the moment. While these things are undoubtedly true, experience tells us that there's no substitute for a good, honest, supportive friend. A group of friends like this has the ability to transform lives. The people you choose to hang out with intimately affects your self of self-worth, shapes your values, and contributes or detracts from your social energy level. A positive, healthy group of friends will dramatically bolster your ability to manifest in your life.

When you are part of a group where all group members have your best interests in mind and view you favorably, you will experience powerful validation as well as a sense of belonging. Humans are made to thrive in groups. Oftentimes, we are forced into positions that do not validate our worth and hinder our ability to consistently create positive thought energy. For example, we may have difficult coworkers that we can't avoid. We may have negative family members. Our significant others may be prone to depression or rumination. It's rare that you'll find a social group where *all* group members are positive and supportive. There's always going to be a few bad apples. The important thing is to identify various groups and their potential benefit to you. When you find the right people, you will find that your manifestation powers are greatly amplified as well as your level of general happiness.

We've already talked about how to identify and mitigate the dangers of negative people in your life. In one of our exercises we identified the negative and the positive people within your life. Now let's look at the groups that you are a member of. Everyone has at least a few groups that they are part of. Work and family groups are the common denominators among people. You might have a few others such as your softball team, church group, or ski club.

About 25 years ago, I left home to join the Army. It was the first time I had lived away from my parents, having just graduated high school. I was a combat medic assigned to a field unit at Ft.Lewis in Washington State. I quickly fell in love with the local area, and I took full advantage of all nature had to offer me there. I was a private in the Army and was very poor. I bought a little Honda Civic clunker off a lemon lot for $600 and used it to explore Washington, Canada, and Northern Oregon. Every weekend I was out somewhere hiking, biking, or skiing. Despite the great adventures I was having, I was completely miserable and lonely. I hardly had any friends, and my Army unit was highly segregated socially along racial lines. I was part of a small medical detachment with about fifty soldiers. The unit was made up primarily of Hispanics and African Americans. There were only two other white soldiers in my unit. Although we all got along fine and eventually became close friends over the years, for the most part, blacks and Hispanics would tend to hang out together which meant that oftentimes we were left out. It was a strange experience to be in the ethnic minority for the first time in my life. These racial divisions were never intentional, but it just worked out that way.

So I found myself in a rather lonely position being 3,000 miles away from family and friends. One of the guys in my unit was into country music and line dancing and I would sometimes go with him to a local country Western club. It was one night there that I met some wonderful friends who greatly helped me through this rough time. Mary and Sara were both Mormons and actively went to church. They invited to attend some church functions with them. They were legitimately nice people and never tried to recruit me to their religion. Their church had a full court basketball court inside, and almost every day there was a pickup game! I started playing basketball there and made a lot of new friends. These people were some of the most caring and supportive individuals I have ever known, and over the few years during my tour they proved to be a constant source of support and friendship. That support network instantly boosted my self-esteem, eliminated my loneliness, and propelled me into greater and greater social success. Their support and encouragement spilled over into my other social groups and my entire life benefited.

Do you have a solid support group? We've discussed already in this book how important it is to identify negative people. Identifying positive people is even more important. Good friends are the best resource you can find and a wonderful source of positive encouragement and support in your life. Sometimes it can be hard however, to find this type of supportive group. In our modern society, people tend to gravitate toward a selfish stance, attempting to arrange everything in their life to suit their purposes. Social media and interconnectedness of communications has reduced our connections to blips of near meaningless chatter. Real friendships can be hard to find through all the egos and ambivalence we have towards one another. Despite the modern challenges we face, it is worth the effort to find a solid group which will support and encourage you.

It's best to find at least *two* groups of solid support so that you don't build reliance on one single group. The dynamic nature of human relations is messy, and redundancy in your support groups is always a good idea. Church is an excellent place to find this sort of group. If you aren't religious though, this can be a problem since the core motivator of the group will be the ideology. Another great place to find a solid support group is by joining a sports team. Coed sports teams are ideal because everyone is included, and you are able to build a diverse set of relationships. Any sort of club that holds a common interests is also a great place to meet people.

The Importance of Social Diversity

It's hard wired into our DNA that we want to hold on to the friends and family we have and build emotional walls around them to protect our tribe. Let's recognize that this is part of our innate character. We shouldn't, however, necessarily accept that this is beneficial to us. Our modern age is riddled with situations and social conditions that we have not properly evolved for biologically speaking. We are fighting against innate tendencies every day. That's ok, but as rational and intelligent beings, it's our job to respond and shape our lives in ways that will bring us the most love and joy. This means that we need to seek out diversity.

You will naturally have a tendency to hang with people who are similar to you. Think about your circle of friends. If you're like most people, you probably have friends who grew up in the same town or state, hold the same religious and political views, or participate in the same sports. It's easy for us to be friends with those whom we share many common interests and beliefs. Seek out friendships with those people who are different from you in some way. If you are a Christian, seek out a friendship with a Muslim. Don't try to change them – fully accept them and make sure they fully accept you as well. Simply attempt to connect as human beings.

The only treatment which can protect us against our innate tendency as humans to exclude and see ourselves as part of the in-group, is by achieving greater and greater levels of mindfulness, coupled with exposure to a diverse set of friends. With mindfulness, we begin to connect to a universal consciousness that is pure love, energy, and inclusion. All living creatures are part of it and once we understand, on a spiritual level that we are truly all the same, it's hard to hate someone just because their skin color is different than ours or because they practice a different religion. True empathy causes lines of nationalism to blur and cultural differences to be celebrated for their uniqueness rather than used to reinforce a sense of disconnection. Mindfulness enables us to view the world and all its inhabitants as a holy place; full of spiritual beings in temporary physical form.

From a state of mindfulness, we can very quickly shift into a state of radical abundance. Not just abundance for ourselves, but for all those whom we come into contact with. There is a limitless supply of joy, happiness, and love available to every individual on this Earth. Harnessing the power of the mind and tapping into the power of the Law of Attraction will very quickly transform your life in beautiful and miraculous ways.

When I started playing soccer as an adult, the men's team I put together consisted of many players from outside of the US. I formed close friendships with my buddy Kutaiba, who is from Saudi Arabia, and my good friend Marwan, who is from Eritrea. Both of these guys are devout Muslims. Being friends with them has taught me so much about their religion and culture, and those friendships have really broken down walls of ignorance that I had held in my mind for so many years. I realized how similar we are, and how, despite our different belief systems, we ultimately are all humans who laugh, cry, and feel the same.

Occasionally, I go to a gospel church service. I'm not particularly religious in any way, but I love the energy and sense of spiritual connection that I get there. Most of the time, me and my girl-friend are the only white people in the church! I love this feeling of being accepted by a group outside my own ethnic bubble of reality. Attending this gospel service has enriched my life im-measurably and helped me progress in my spiritual journey. The first time I went, I felt very nervous. I felt like an outsider. After the service, when so many people came up to me and gave me a hug or shook my hand and welcomed me to their church, I felt an overwhelming sense of peace and love. Pushing yourself outside your social bubble will bring you immense benefits.

It's up to you to engineer your social support system. Work the exercise at the end of this chapter to create a rich, supportive, and loving social life. When we actively seek out diversity in our lives, we learn so much about ourselves – we learn about our own ig-norance, social class, and unearned privilege and most important of all, we learn that we are *all* the same at a fundamental level. **Diverse friendships knock down walls of hatred and intolerance and replace them with feelings of connection and love.**

Another benefit of seeking diverse social networks is that you are never too dependent on any one group. People are fallible and will let you down in many situations. If we follow the princi-ple of never expecting too much from others then we won't be disappointed. Love people despite their character flaws. I have friends who are perpetually late. I even have friends who consis-tently cancel plans at the last minute. I don't write these friends off – I simply recognize that this person has this personality trait and am aware that they will likely continue to act in this way. Rather than attempting to change them, I lower my expecta-tions, work around their behavior, and accept them fully as they are. The only time you should disconnect from someone is if they are actively a negative influence in your life. Refer to the previous chapter which covers this to identify these types. For most peo-ple however, simply lowering your expectations and practicing acceptance will work great.

Having many different social networks means that you will receive support and encouragement from multiple sources, and you've also got some redundancy built in. If one group turns toxic, or starts to make you feel drained, you have other groups which can provide the supportive social energy you need to thrive.

So to recap, here's a list of places where you might be able to find a super supportive group of people. Just make sure that whatever group you join is full of people who are honest, reliable, and are not haters. Haters exist everywhere, but are more common in people who engage in a lot of social comparison and in individuals who are strongly egoistic. It's fine to be in groups with people like this, but never rely on them as a primary means of support. If you do so, your life and manifestation goals will be severely restricted. Stick to groups where you feel welcomed, supported, accepted, and appreciated for who you are. Some examples:

Church groups

Sports Teams

Writing Clubs

Art/ Urban Sketching clubs

Home brewing Clubs

Sewing clubs

Political parties that hold your same views

Volunteer groups

Non-Profit Organizations

Amnesty International Groups

Extended family gatherings

Support Groups

EXERCISE 15

The goal of this exercise is to identify your current social support groups and to strengthen or replace those as needed.

On a piece of paper or in your journal, make a list of the top three social groups you are currently a member of. This could be things such as ski club, church groups, sports teams, or hobby clubs. It can also be less organized groups such as childhood friends, friends from work, etc.

List your top three social groups in one column on the left hand side of the paper. Next to each, answer the follow question: *"Does this group support and enhance my life in positive ways?"*

If you answered NO for any of your groups listed, think about limiting your interaction with that group. Also, take a moment to brainstorm a replacement for negative groups and commit to a plan of action. Write your action plan in the third column. An example action plan might be: Join bowling team, Call Susan about joining her cooking club, etc.

Chapter 24: LOA Amplifier: Focus on Death

"Decay is inherent in all component things." – The Buddha

Death is something that most people rarely think about. We naturally tend to value the permanent things in our lives over the fleeting. We like to imagine that the strong bonds of family and friends will last forever. We all know that we die, and that all our loved ones will die as well, but we just don't like to confront it head on. Many people act as if they are somehow exempt from death and choose to operate as if they have all the time in the world. The reality is that death is always around us. If you pay attention, you'll see the signs of death everywhere.

The irony here is that the impermanence of things is what makes life so beautiful. In the Old Testament book of Proverbs it says that man's life is like a flower, briefly blooming and then quickly wilting away. The one truth about reality that we know to be true is that everything is in a constant state of change. Our time here is finite. Every physical object in the world is decaying. Even the Earth itself is on a course to die. Every tree, plant, dog, bird, etc. that you see will be gone one day. If all this is causing a sense of depression, it's only because you're clinging to the fallacy of permanence. Being surrounded by death is a cause for celebration. Recognizing death will alter your thinking in radical ways and help you to create an intentional, deliberate life.

When you initially allow yourself to contemplate and face your own mortality, you may feel inclined to wish for some future state which guarantees you immortality. Perhaps if you're a technologist, you may cling to the hope that science will provide an answer to the problem of death. Among young people, conversations about death tend to circle back to this comment: *"I'm sure that by the time we get that old they'll have something figured out."* Then there's talk of cloning organs, printing organs with a 3d bio-printer, uploading our consciousness to a computer, etc. For religious folks, most belief systems provide a ready man answer to the problem of death. Christians can look forward to heaven, Buddhists can look forward to starting the cycle over again as a reincarnated being, and Islamists get to spend eternity in a mansion in paradise having lots of great sex. Although thoughts of an afterlife provide us with a sense of solace, it's fleeting and not accurate. Believing in immortality prevents us from confronting the true nature of our existence and blinds us the incredible beauty present in every single moment. Every breath we take is an amazing experience. Every conversation we share with another person is so precious. We when start to come to terms with the fragility and finite state inherent to human existence, we start to truly appreciate the magic and wonder of the present moment.

People who Think about Death are More Alive

By thinking about death, you actually become *more* alive. Acknowledging death and change completely transforms our perspective and the way we look at the world. Let's examine how thinking about death benefits our lives:

Your Perspective Changes

Do you ever look at a beautiful flower and imagine that it'll be unchanged in two weeks? Part of the appreciation you have for a flower lies in the fact that you understand how temporary it is.

Knowing that its beauty will soon come to an end makes it that much more beautiful. When we start to look at the moments of our life this way, things tend not to bother us as much. Traffic jams become wonderful opportunities to listen to an audio book or to call a friend to talk. Moments that bored or annoyed us in the past become incredible celebrations of life. Many people are constantly in a hurry to get somewhere else. Once they're there, they almost immediately start to look for the next best place to be. Knowing that your time is finite makes every moment amazing. Even a simple walk through the woods with your dog becomes a cherished experience. When you think of all that had to work out for every moment of your existence to happen, those moments become infinitely more significant. Along with this, you'll feel a deep peace as you realize that right now, in this place, you are exactly where you need to be. Looking at the world through the lens of mortality allows things to slow down and for your heart to open to the gratitude that accepting the present moment brings.

You Become Motivated

Much of our motivations originate in the desire to maintain favorable states or to potentially increase our position or place in the world. Many people take incremental action toward the realization of their dreams out of sheer fear and doubt. If you *know* that you're going to die, and that you have a finite amount of time to make things happen, you'll care less about fear and care more about action. Want to write a book? Be famous? Climb a mountain? Learn to play guitar? Reconnect with your lost love or estranged friend? All these things start to look different when we really understand that fear is an irrational roadblock of our own making. Fear is dependent amount you caring about the outcome. If you know your time is finite, you'll care less about outcomes and just go ahead and give it a shot. You've got nothing to lose!

Since we are just here for a short while, why not try everything you've ever wanted to do? Why stay in a shitty job or relation-ship? You're going to die my friend, and the more you focus on that, the more you will respect and value your *own* time. Re-specting your own time means that you spend it wisely and that you could care less about those who tried to put you down or sidetrack you from the realization of your goals.

Exercise 16

Every morning, after you are done running through your grati-tude exercises, throw in a reminder about your own mortality as a reminder of the finite nature of your existence.

As an affirmation, say the following statement aloud: *"I know that my life is finite and my every moment is a precious gift from the universe. I celebrate and embrace my day. I choose to celebrate the incredible beauty in every moment of my day."*

CHAPTER 25: PUTTING IT ALL TOGETHER: A BOOT CAMP PROGRAM FOR AN ABUNDANT LIFE

So we've learned all this incredible information about the Law of Attraction and the radical and amazing benefits that directed and inspired action can bring to our lives. At this point, you can choose to implement what you want, following your own time schedule. For some this may be easy. For others who may be mired in years of negative thinking, bad habits, negative relationships, or poor physical health, you may need a boot camp of sorts. This final chapter is set up to provide you just that.

In this chapter, you will find a template for living that you can use for the next 30 days. I guarantee that if you follow this template for 30 days you will see dramatic and incredible positive changes occur in your life. Use this 30 days period as a trial to see how you feel, what you can handle, and how easily you can incorporate action into your life. Get ready for massive and sustained change and a consciously lived life full of intention and possibilities!

First, we need to establish some principles to follow during this 30 day Law of Attraction boot camp challenge. By establishing these in the beginning, you will know what to expect and start to think about how you can pull this off. The power is within you. Don't hesitate – think, act and manifest.

Principle 1: Love Yourself. Everything, and I mean everything, that we do in this program revolves around the idea that you are absolutely 100% in love with **you**. Embrace and accept every aspect of yourself as you go through this process. Understand that the actions of your past don't define your future but, at the same time, you should be very grateful for your past because it has formed you and brought to this point. You are a spiritual being, destined for growth. You are exactly where and who you need to be at this moment. The universe created you out of love, and you are love in a physical form. I'm not asking for you to be selfish throughout this process, but I am asking you to love yourself first and foremost.

Principle 2: Wake Early - By waking earlier than normal every day you will have time to complete the actions necessary to move you into an abundant state of mind. We need extra time in the morning to reflect, gain our composure, and ready our minds for the day ahead. Living a consciously aware day is exciting and intense – only through early morning preparation can we harness all there is to offer.

Principle 3: Eliminate Dangerous Diversions - This can be a tough one to swallow at first but if you want radical positive change, it must be done. This means that you cut out any diversion that takes you out of reality. You should know by now what these are from completing the exercises in this book. If you haven't identified your own dangerous diversions, go back to Chapter 12 and complete the exercise at the end of the chapter. Some very common dangerous diversions are alcohol consumption and excessive TV watching. You will undoubtedly have times during the 30 day period when you will want to revert back to a particular dangerous diversion. Alcohol, for example, has the tendency to numb our emotions over time. This occurs even for social drinkers. Many who eliminate alcohol find that suddenly they start to feel emotions more intensely. For some, this is too much to handle and they may seek the solace of alcohol once again. If you slip up during this period, don't put much thought into it. Simply acknowledged that you slipped back into your old escapism and continue with the 30 days as if it never happened.

Principle 4: Create a Master TO-DO List - By creating this list and using it daily to direct your work flow, you will have a guide and a metric by which you can see your progress. If you find yourself distracted or struggling to continue the program, you can always go back to your master to do list and get busy. Remember though that having a to-do list is just a guide. Rather than focusing on outcomes, focus on directed action. Just use your master to-do as a loose reference. When we focus on to-do lists we are usually focusing on outcomes, and this can be de-motivating. Progress is made along a continuous course, not through the completion of set tasks you write on a piece of paper or plug into an app. For example, if one of your goals on your master to-do list is to clean your house top to bottom, you could take a task completion approach and clean the bathroom, then clean the kitchen, etc. until you reach your goal. A more effective approach is to set a timer for one hour, and just clean. Don't worry about outcomes, just focus on the process. Outcomes are simply a by-product of taking action.

Principle 5: Take time to Relax - Here's where many people have to redefine what they mean by relaxing. For many, their idea of relaxing is settling down on the couch with a bag of chips and binge watching episodes of Orange is the New Black. This, as you know, is actually a dangerous diversion because it's an unconscious activity that serves as an escape from ourselves. Learn to relax with ACE - activities of conscious engagement. An example might be meditation, taking a walk in the woods with your significant other, or just reading a book. Laugher is important.

Don't take any of this too seriously. Try to find humor in everything. If you identified TV watching as a dangerous diversion, lay off it for a few weeks. After that, you can occasionally watch TV with one objective in mind: to laugh your ass off. Watch something silly and funny, which will generate positive vibrations. This state will be sustained throughout the following day, and your interactions with others will be more fun and lighthearted. Humor makes everything easier.

Principle 6: Be open to the universe. Being open to the universe means that throughout the boot camp program you will be willing and ready to receive instruction for inspired action. Don't worry about how you will receive that instruction. As long as you are doing the daily actions outlined in the program, you will naturally shift to an abundant mindset. Your mind will open and become sensitive to the signs and calling the universe provides. Listening to these subtle messages will result in beautiful changes that can happen overnight.

For the next 30 days, commit to the following schedule. Depending on your work situation, you may need to shift some times around. As long as you complete the daily actions, you will see results.

Principle 7: Always assume positive intent. This may be the most important principle to keep during your boot camp. Assuming positive intent means that you are intentionally creating a mind bias in order to bring positive and supportive people into your life. Initially, this isn't natural. As previously discussed, we are not hard-wired genetically to give people the benefit of the doubt. It takes time to fully develop this mind bias hack, and a few people have reported to me that it took them over a year to do so. Use the next 30 days to constantly reinforce this belief, and you will see that soon it becomes easier to maintain.

The following is an example of a self-imposed boot camp day. Adjust as needed to your needs and ability. You know yourself best, so impose a program that is challenging yet doable.

0500 – Wake

0530 — Cardiovascular exercise

0615 – Give thanks for what you have and for what's ahead. Focus on truly feeling grateful. Use written affirmations if needed.

0630- 0645 – Meditate. Allow yourself to freely experience your emotional state. Use the green blob of emotion exercise from chapter 3 if needed.

0700 ~ 1600 – this time is generally reserved for your work or career. When working, use your master to-do list as a guideline to stay productive. Throughout your workday, take a break every 2 hours to close your eyes and *feel* intensely grateful. Also take this time to *feel* the *'feelings of having it now'* for whatever you wish to manifest into your life.

- Practice smiling and complimenting your co-workers.

- As you go throughout your day, consciously strive to see the good in your co-workers and your boss. Always assume positive intent!

- Listen to positive or inspiring LoA podcasts during your commute.

1600 - ACE + Positive Social Engagement. Every day, fill your after work time with ACE. There are lots of solo ACE such as playing guitar and writing a short story. This is fine and you will see results with this. However, always try to add a social element to all your activities of conscious engagement. Instead of mountain biking by yourself, call a friend. Join a book club. Also, joining an intramural or recreational sports league is a great way to accomplish this. Soccer, softball, curling, or tennis – whatever you find an interest in, as long as it's not an escapism and allows you to connect socially with others, this is good. Keeping your environment clean and orderly is important as well, so you will find that you can't always add in positive social engagement. Do so as time permits.

On weekends, follow the same morning routines but slam the entire day full of ACE + Positive Social Engagement. This is *your* time to live consciously, so take time to plan your weekends in advance. Camping trips with friends, cleaning your house, doing your laundry, listening to Law of Attraction podcasts, reading an engaging book, and going to church are all examples of ACE that you can fill your weekend with. The biggest danger on a weekend or whenever we have time away from work is that we can easily just lay around and do nothing. This too, is a dangerous diversion. Choose to fill your day with activities of conscious engagement. This doesn't mean that you need to run yourself ragged. To the contrary, take breaks to decompress in your own way.

Be Prepared for Inspired Action

Along the way, be ready to change course at any minute when the universe sends you a hint. This is when you should recognize the info as an incredible gift, and move directly into inspired action. As you know, inspired action is the fastest and most powerful way to manifest something positive in your life.

Seek out Law of attraction literature to read throughout your day. Listening to audio programs and podcasts on positive thinking are helpful as well. Engage your mind with *only* positive things. During your boot camp, and during your regular day to day life, it's critical that you focus *only* the positive things in life.

Conclusion

The life you want is in your hands. You have the ability to transcend the confines of the false limitations society and your own limiting beliefs have imposed on you. Whatever you dream, you can achieve. **What you think, you will become.** I hope that this book has helped you to start or continue living a deliberate life, where you are actively and consciously creating your own reality as you go along. When you apply the Law of Attraction, along with all the pragmatic advice this book has provided, you will see results beyond your most hopeful aspirations.

You came from the universe as stardust, and through time you've been part of cycle of life that has culminated in the ultimate expression of the universe - intelligent and conscious life. As a beautiful expression of the universe, you have the ability to act creatively to define your own reality. No matter what condition or situation you started from, you *now* have the knowledge and power to rewrite your life as only you desire.

Post Script: Evidence for the Law of Attraction

The Law of Attraction throughout History

The Maxims of Ptahhotep

The earliest known written evidence of the Law of Attraction can be found in the ancient Egyptian writings known as The Maxims of Ptahhotep, from the year 2375 BC. It was written by a subject of the Egyptian king during the Fifth Dynasty named Ptahhotep. He wrote the book at an advanced age as a collection of wise advice and stories about human behavior that he could pass down to his son before he died. It was Ptahhotep's culmination of a lifetime of pondering and dealing with hardships that motivated him to document all that he had learned. He felt compelled to pass down the secrets of life to his son, in order to spare him the hard lessons he had experienced in his own life.

Some of the primary messages in The Maxims of Ptahhotep deal with the importance of developing an attitude of truthfulness, self-control, and kindness to others. He also expressly condemns open conflict and aggressive behavior. Examining the text, we can see many examples where he advises his son to seek an attitude of abundance, and to put faith in God or the universe to achieve his aims.

Let's examine the most significant lines from the translated text:

"The human race never accomplishes anything. It's what God commands that gets done." - Here he is telling his son to have faith in the universe and let the "how" be handled by God.

"If you work hard, and if growth takes place as it should in the fields, it is because God has placed abundance in your hands." - Essentially he is saying that abundance is an inherent gift from God, and that only through nurturing an attitude of abundance can we grow into something great.

"Those who[m] the Gods guide cannot get lost. Those they forbid passage will not be able to cross the river of life." - Only by embracing the power of a universal source of abundance can we realize our greatest gifts and goals in life. When we shut down through logical reasoning and cynicism, we can never achieve what others deem impossible.

The Yajurvedo

The ancient Sanskrit text, the Yajurvedo, from around 1000 BC, was written by Vedic priests as a set of instructions performed over a ritual fire called a yajna fire. In these ancient instructions, we find evidence that the priests understood the power of one's thought energy, and the ways in which our thoughts can determine future events. In the following text, the word Savita can be thought of as a reference to the universe. Savita was a Vedic deity that literally means Sun.

First harnessing the mind, Savita; creating thoughts and perceiving light, brought Agni from the earth.

Harnessing the gods with mind; they who go with thought to the sky, to heaven, Savita instigates those who will make great light.

With the mind harnessed, we are instigated by god Savita, for strength to go to heaven.

In this passage, the Vedic priests are telling us that in order to achieve greatness in life, we must first harness and control our minds. *"Harnessing the gods with mind"* is explicitly telling us today what they knew over 1000 years ago – by controlling our thought energies, we can tap into a source of limitless abundance.

The Tree of Life

The Tree of Life is an ancient symbol used by the Jewish Kabbalists as a method to understand existence and reality. In it, we find strong connections to what we now call the Law of Attraction. The Tree of Life is an extremely complex heuristic structure consisting of ten separate spiritual principles. These principles work interchangeably between one another to explain the origins and continued existence of the universe.

Consciousness in the Kabbalah is viewed as a wonderful gift emanating from the physical world, which we can use as an instrument to tap into the limitless abundance of a universal power. Their view is that this universal, limitless power that we call the universe is actually expressing itself in the form of a finite physical entity. In other words, **you are the universe in human form.** The

Kaballlah also infers that energy condenses into matter and back again. Understanding yourself and the material world in which you temporarily reside is the goal of the Tree of Life – specifically, understanding that all physical forms including your own mind are made from energy. We have the ability to tap into that energy and direct the outcome of our physical reality.

The Law of Attraction in Chinese Medicine

In the 1970s, Grandmaster Dr. Ming Pang created a new system of Chinese medicine known as Qigong. A peculiar aspect of this form of Chinese medicine is that it does not involve the use of any chemical or herbal substances. Instead, healing of disease states is achieved through the harnessing of thought and spirit energy. In Qigong, there are 6 steps, or "Golden Keys" through which one can obtain healing. The process is remarkably similar to the processes and practices we use with the Law of Attraction to manifest our desires. Qigong uses the power of the mind to heal and restore the body. It is another form of the Law of Attraction that is primarily focused on healing rather than the manifestation of people or things. When we look at the six golden keys, we can see many elements of the Law of Attraction in practice:

1. Haola - daily mantra meaning "All is Well" (gratitude exercises)

2. Inner Smile - allowing oneself to draw out deep feelings of happiness (meditation/mindfulness)

3. Love and Service (like attracts like)

4. Trust and Belief (Step 2)

5. The Chi Field (harnessing positive vibrational energy)

6. Diligent Practice (Maintaining and Adjusting)

Made in the USA
San Bernardino, CA
16 July 2018